draw

up your game
with professional
graphic facilitation skills

LISE GRASTRUP

Author: Lise Grastrup

Book coach: Malene Bendtsen
Cover and book layout: Diren Yardimli
Illustrations: Lise Grastrup

ISBN: 9788740451221

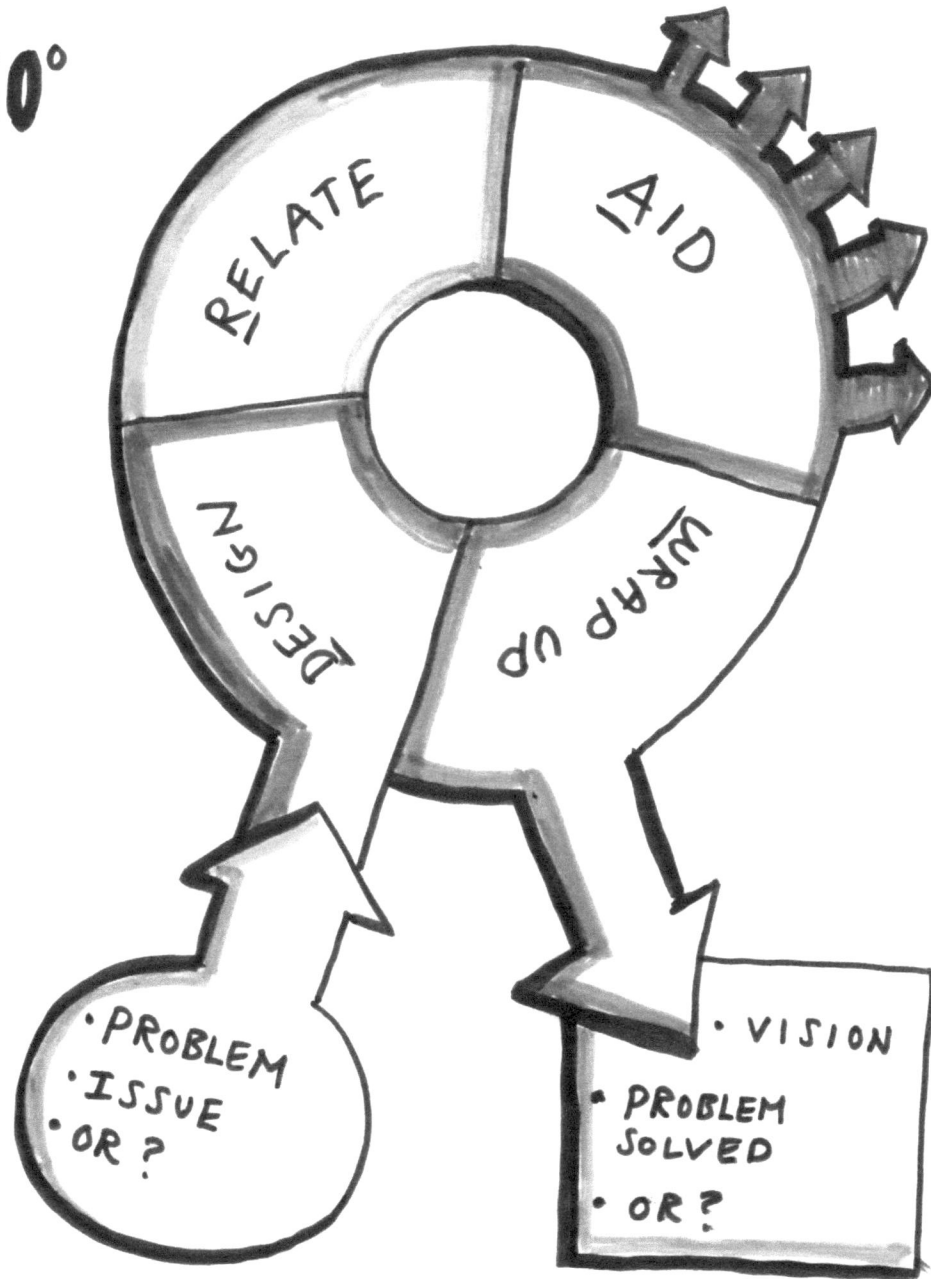

DRAW 360°

RELATE

AID

DESIGN

WRAP UP

- PROBLEM
- ISSUE
- OR ?

- VISION
- PROBLEM SOLVED
- OR ?

table of contents

intro

introduction

introduction

This book is about drawing and why we all ought to do it. In childhood, most people were able to draw, and though many adults forget, how we admire those who can still draw as adults. But everybody can learn to draw (again) and you can, too!

About the book

The focus of this book is on the professional use of drawing and making you a better, more interesting graphic recorder, facilitator, meeting leader, or teacher.

The book examines the mental barriers built up against drawing and explains why we should do it anyway.

It teaches anyone how to draw simple icons and templates and illustrate situations, events, stories, and feelings graphically.

It explains why graphical presentations have a positive impact on our ability to think, analyze, be creative, remember, and feel. It makes the use of graphical elements an obvious choice in your work life.

In the last part of the book, we focus on bringing your new skills into action. We explore a variety of ways to use the tools and guidelines to become an even better facilitator and communicator.

Graphic facilitation is not about pretty drawings, nor are they pieces of art. It is about initiating internal and external dialogue and communicating in an ancient yet new way.

The discovery of magic powers

It was by coincidence that I discovered the incredible and unbeatable superpowers of graphic facilitation. I am an architect, and someone asked me to facilitate by drawing at a meeting in the company I worked for.

Without ever having heard about graphic facilitation before, I put a piece of paper on the wall and started drawing what I heard in the meeting. Quite daunting but also great fun!

I drew the people present at the meeting and all the comments, great ideas, and points made. I drew a visual resume of what happened and what was concluded.

I was amazed at how significant the experience was to the participants and to me. The creative approach was not only fun but had a huge impact on the outcome.

Participants were interested in learning the skills to facilitate using graphic elements. After the meeting, I realized I had obtained a unique position in the company, having added something admirable to my personal brand. I was the girl who could draw with such a great impact!

All of this happened even though the drawing was a bit of a mess and not beautiful in a traditional sense, with icons and text in a hotchpotch, lacking any structure. Nevertheless, people recognized themselves in the drawing, had a lot of fun, and benefited highly from the process. They loved it!

An idea for a business and a life as an independent graphic recorder and teacher was soon born.

If you want more

This book will guide you in building your toolbox of graphical elements and combining them in unique ways to convey your message and add magic to processes in professional contexts.

You can supplement this book with the free workbook and other training material on my website: lisegrastrup.com.

Have fun and try not to think too much or be too critical towards yourself – just go ahead and do it!

Lise Grastrup

Get the free workbook!

www.lisegrastrup.com/draw

To book Lise for a company drawing:

www.lisegrastrup.com/contact

why

graph

graphic communication

16 superpowers of graphic communication

Drawings are a powerful tool for various purposes. Here are some of the ways you will receive your return on investment. But I would love to hear if you experience other benefits (www.lisegrastrup.com).

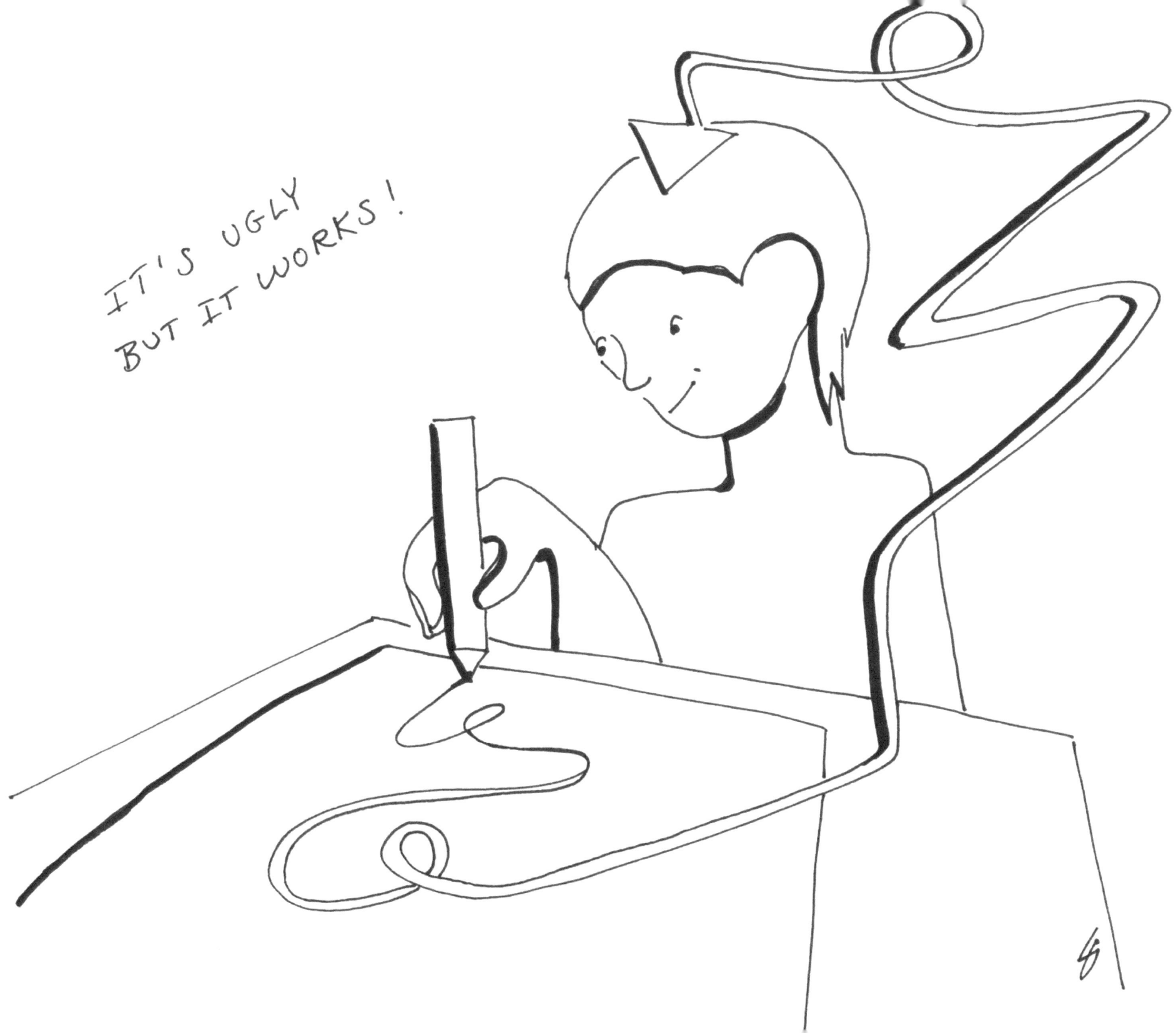

memory enhancing

What we see sticks. Brains love drawings, and we remember things a lot better when we draw it.

Jeffrey Wammes, a Ph.D. candidate at the Department of Psychology at the University of Waterloo in Canada, conducted a study in cooperation with fellow Ph.D. candidate Melissa Meade and professor Myra Fernandes about the powers of drawing, testing it on a group of students:

"We discovered a significant recall advantage for words that were drawn as compared to those that were written. Participants often recalled more than twice as many drawn than written words. We labeled this benefit 'the drawing effect,' which refers to this distinct advantage of drawing words relative to writing them out."

Priscilla Frank writes in her article in 'Culture and Art' from September 2016: "According to research by Jeffrey Wammes and his team at the University of Waterloo in Canada, drawing may be the most reliable way to enhance memory. And it doesn't matter how good or truly horrendous your doodles look – just the very art of sketching them out can help embed them right into your memory bank. Researchers dubbed their findings, published in The Quarterly Journal of Experimental Psychology, 2016, - The drawing effect."

According to American cognition and education scientist, David Hyerle, our brain is able to record 36,000 visual pictures per hour, and at least 70% of all the information we perceive happens through sight, and it happens extremely quickly!

David Hyerle says that our brain is meant to understand the world and create meaning through mapping and constructing patterns and connections. For some reason, we have built a world that is based largely on words and numbers and linear thinking, even though we are much stronger in understanding and learning through visual patterns and pictures.

And something else to think about: when we connect pictures with words in new and surprising ways, we create and fortify synapses and connections in our brain (Donald Hebb). Activating different parts of the brain makes sense.

abstract language

The spoken language and the written language are more fixed and linear, whereas the visual language communicated through illustrations is more fluid, continually developing, constantly inviting new ideas, and new processes.

The visual language is an organic kind of language that is not fixed but very flexible and easy to relate to. Graphics when kept symbolic without too many details, allow for some degree of interpretation.

They are conversation starters and mandate new ways of thought and interpretation. Moreover, the abstract liberates airing thoughts on a general, non-personal level.

You will find that people tell you something you did not think to ask them because of your drawing – or theirs.

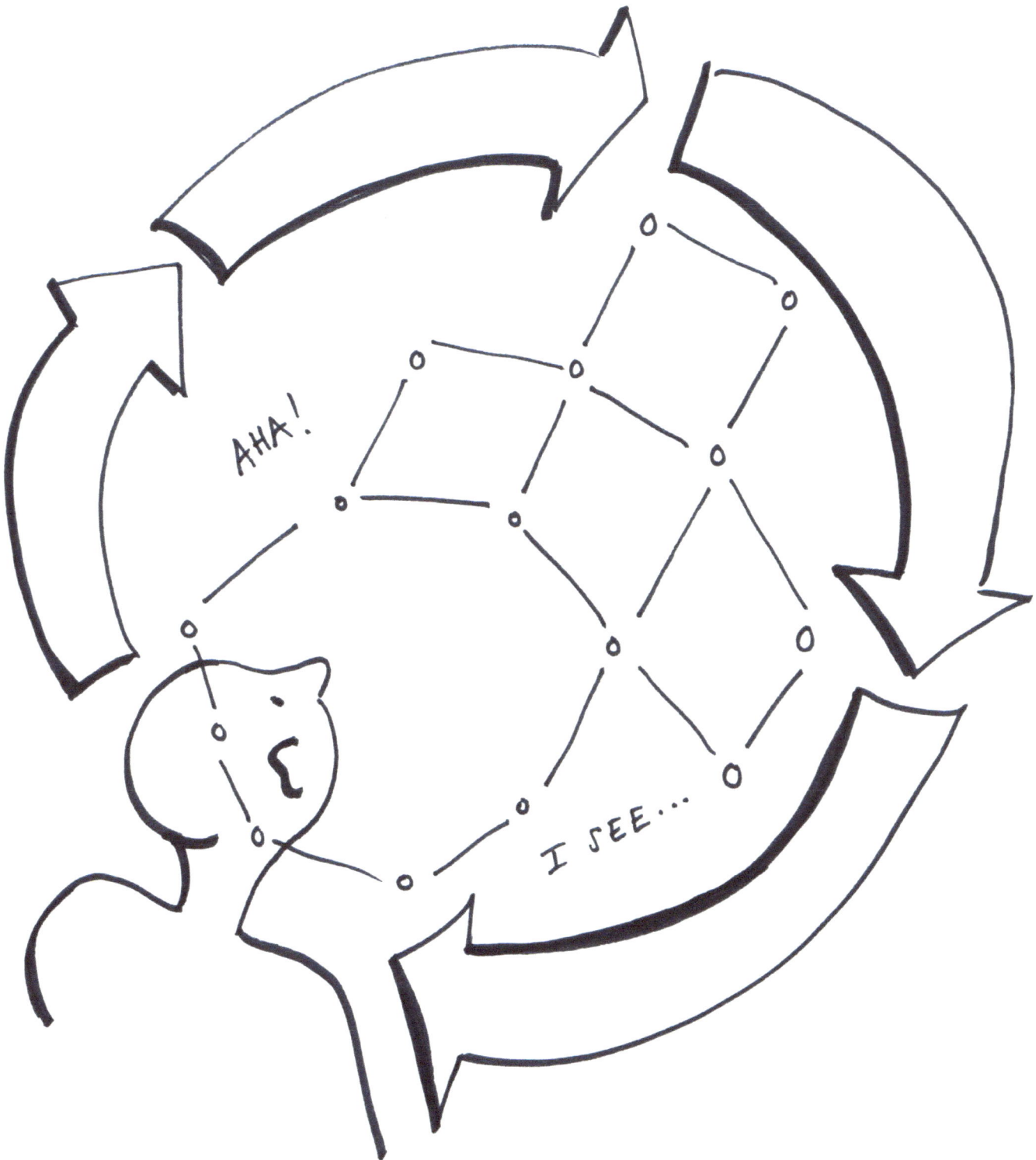

path to the subconscious mind

We are born to mimic what we see, and drawings were our first common non-verbal language as human beings. A drawing sometimes communicates more clearly how we look at the world around us. Engaging people through drawing is easy. While drawing, we can make tangible a pre-born thought that is still not possible to articulate in words.

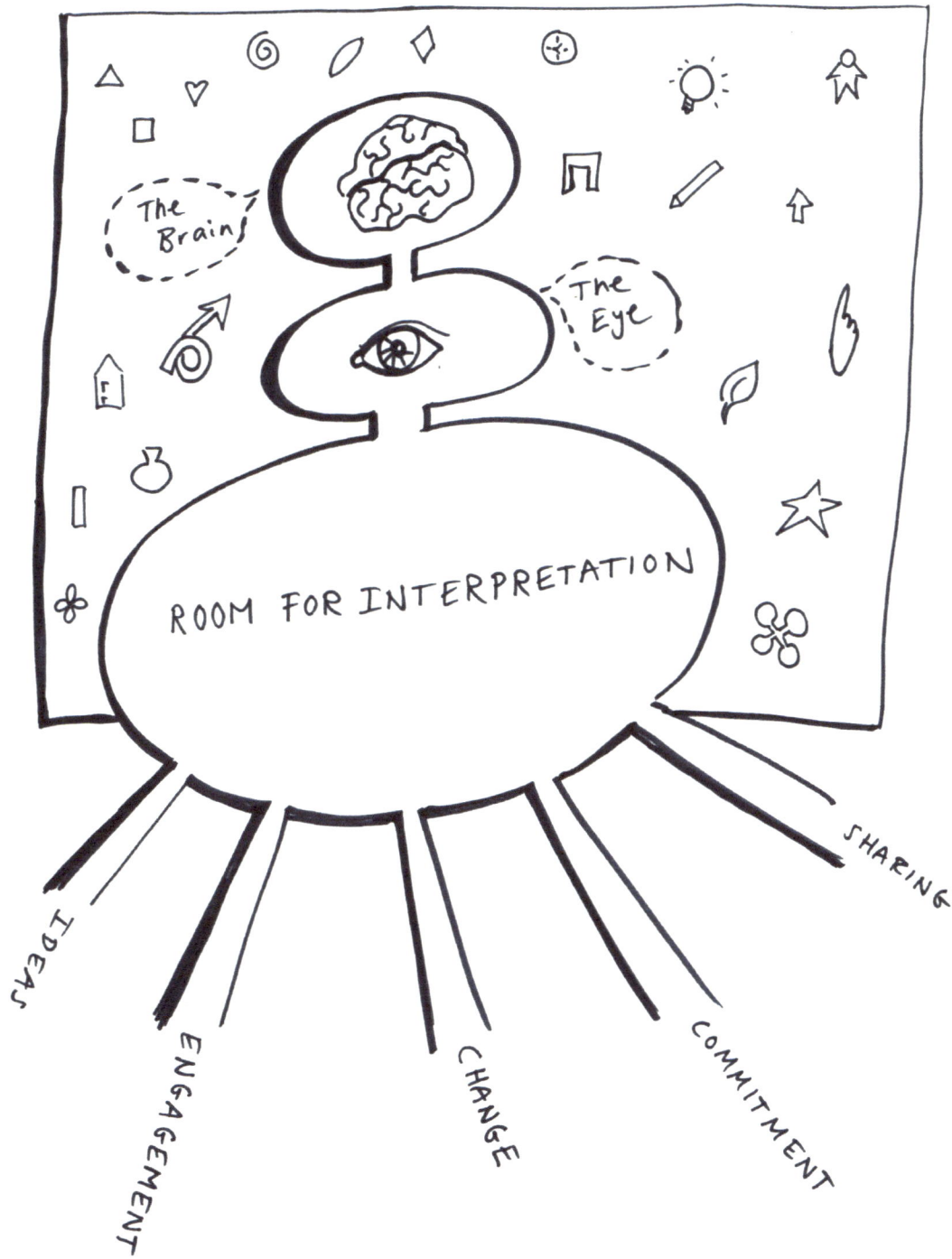

appreciation tool

Drawing what I hear you say is impossible without paying attention and listening carefully to what you are looking to express. As a graphic facilitator or recorder, you are naturally present, and it shows in a powerful way that you take people seriously, and you see what is going on. Literally, you make people feel seen and heard.

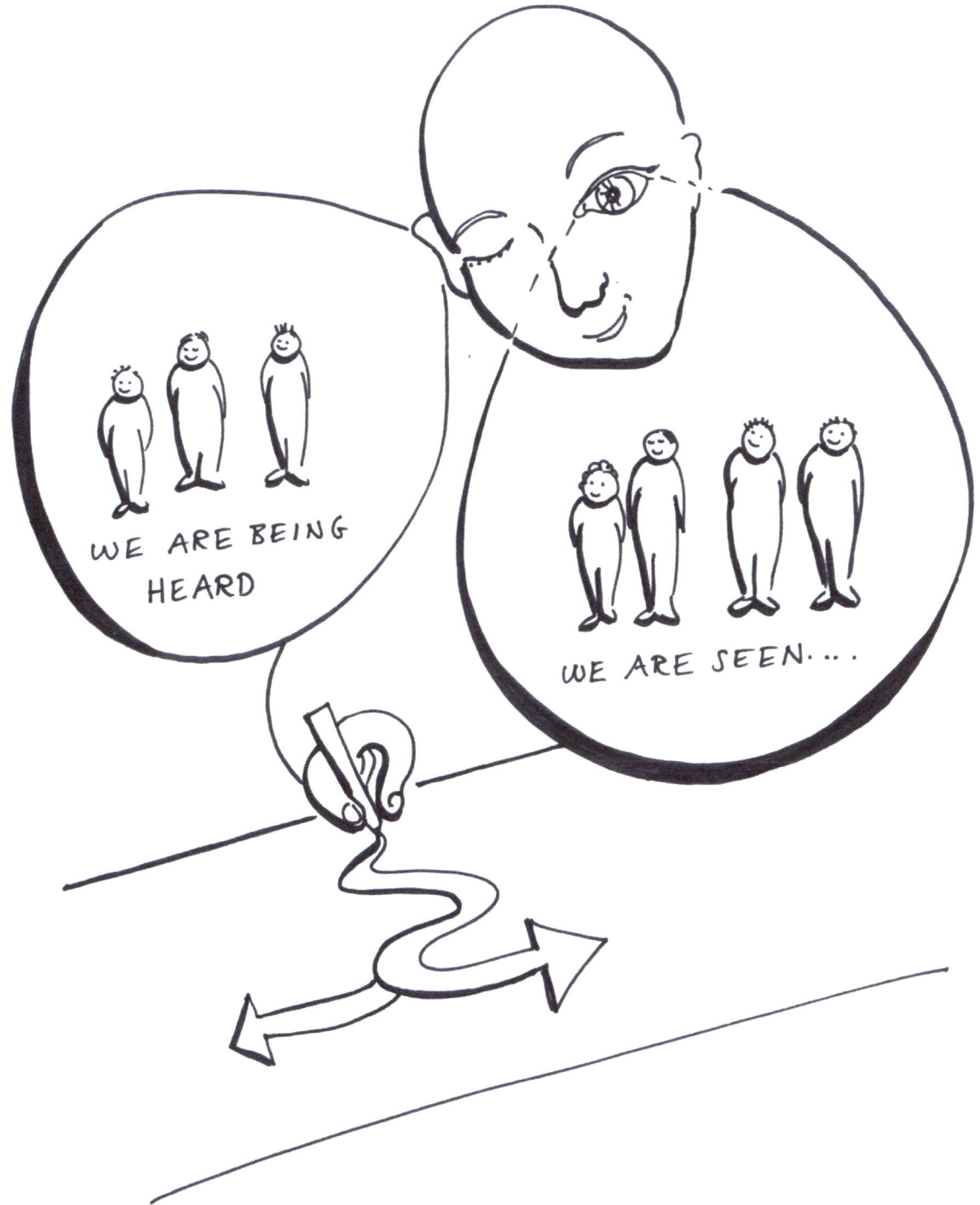

humor

You can add humor purposely to make events, meetings, and other learning moments more lively, joyful, fun, and memorable. Even if entertaining by coincidence, participants will appreciate the opportunity to make fun of

mistakes and misinterpret intentionally.

This raises everyone's spirits while giving the mandate for others to fail, laugh together, and still appreciate one another. Once we show that we are all insecure, we become equal.

idea generation

When drawing, you activate more parts of your brain and in different ways. You connect dots differently, and by stimulating more impulses through various channels, it becomes easier to relate to (complex) information and hold on to thoughts. Ideas can, thus, be developed much faster.

Idea generation is a whole brain sport. You miss out on excellent brain work if you stick to speaking and writing. The left side of the brain is mainly the logical side and to a large extent, the judge of what makes sense or not. The right side is the holistic, creative, and visual side, which we use when drawing or seeing visuals.

The right side does not judge.

faster learning

Images talk to us in a more immediate, direct, and emotional way than words alone. They have the power to create strong feelings and give a first-hand impression of a situation before we are even aware of it and before we have a description in words.

According to Robert E. Horn, people can easily tune in on a subject and relate quickly to the context. In other words, drawing facilitates a direct connection between our feelings and the subconsciousness, which leads to faster learning.

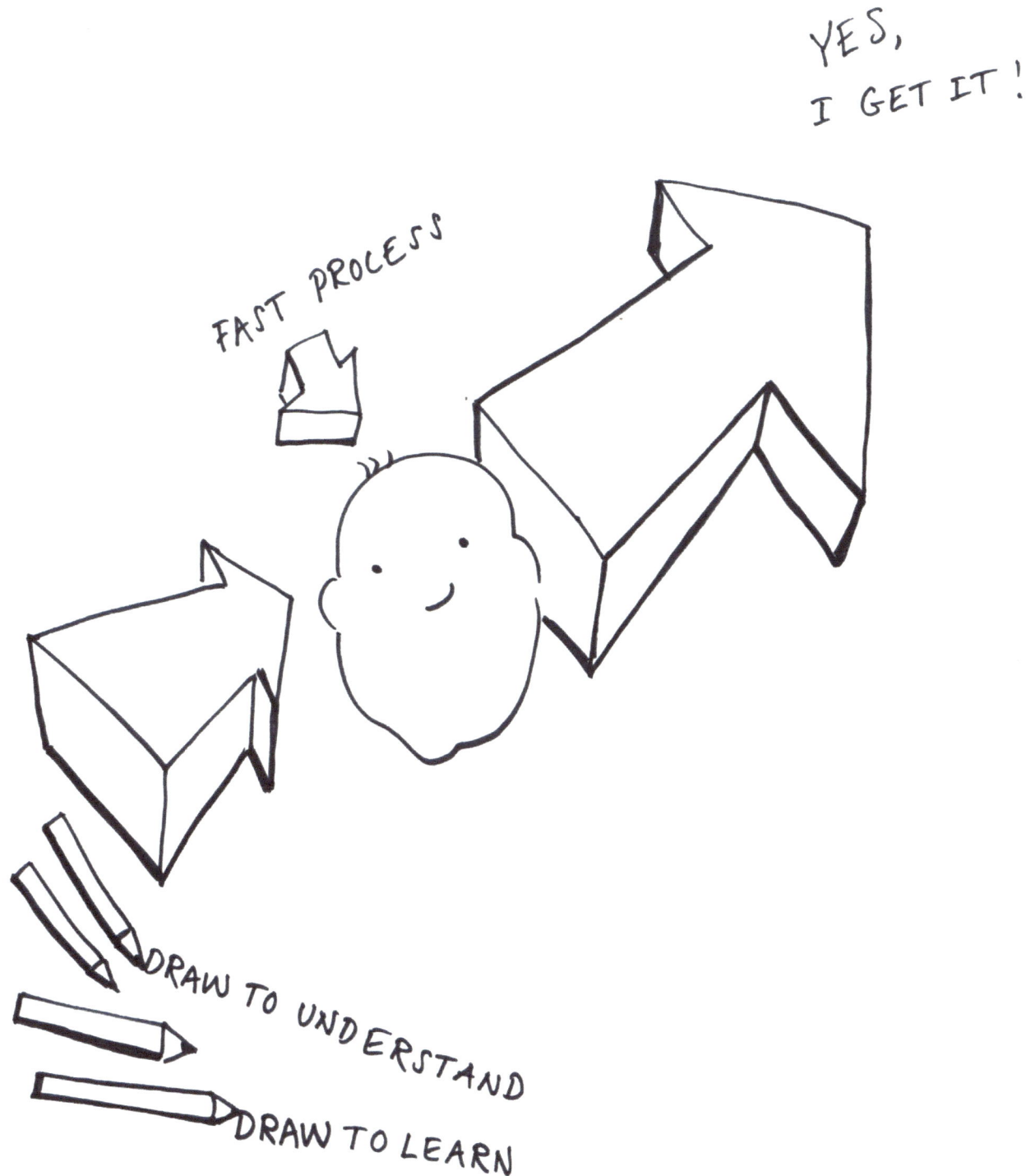

YES,
I GET IT!

FAST PROCESS

DRAW TO UNDERSTAND

DRAW TO LEARN

common ownership

Human beings have a powerful desire to find solutions and to create. Human beings are designers from birth! On top of that, we strive to belong to a herd – to be part of and accepted by a group. Graphic facilitation can combine the two forces and create common ownership for the outcome of a process (i.e., a strategy process).

Even if you are doing all the drawing, the participants are co-creators, and they share the experience of having seen it come to life. They are co-owners.

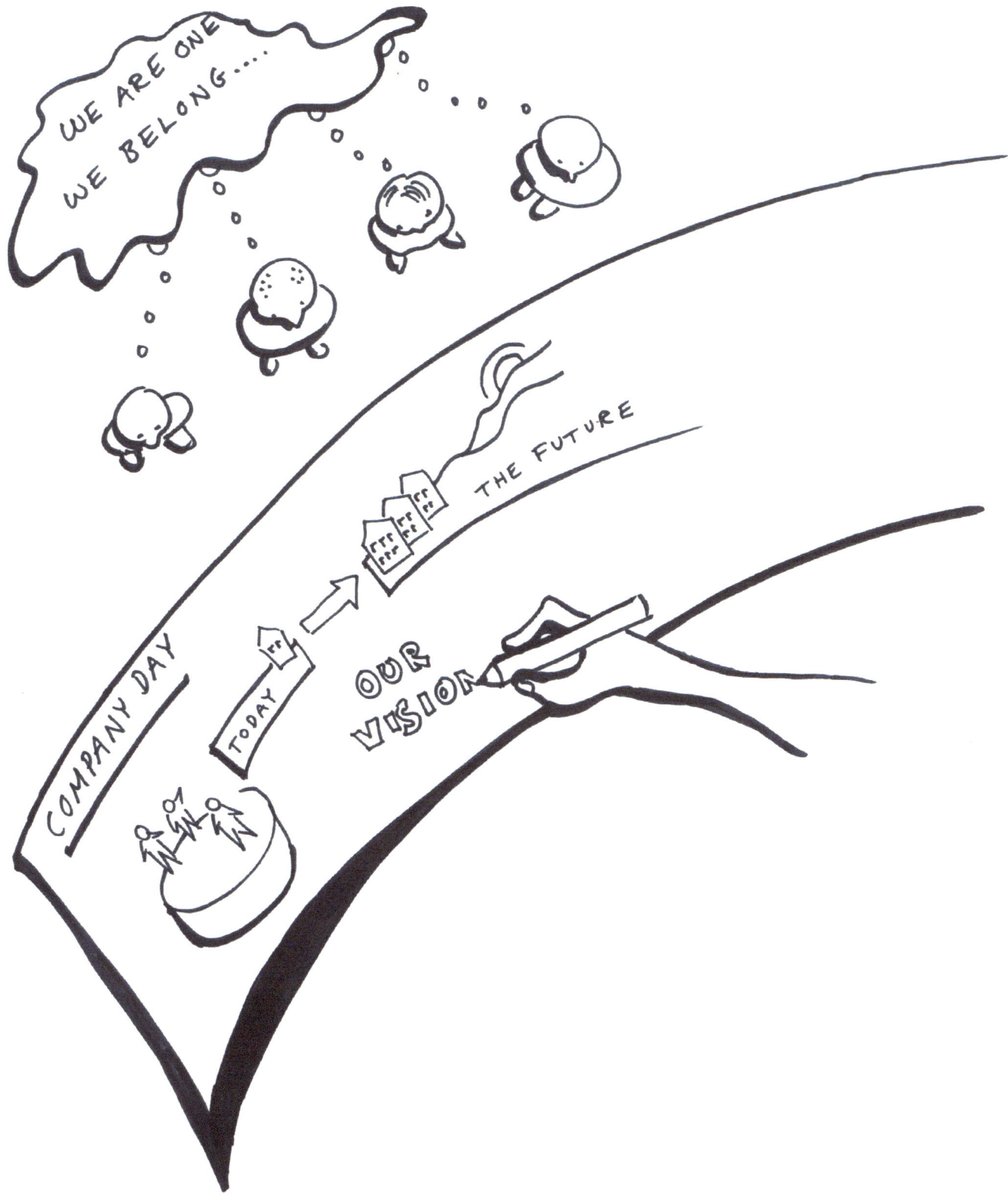

WE ARE ONE
WE BELONG....

THE FUTURE

COMPANY DAY

TODAY

OUR VISION

clarity

Having a conversation about how to illustrate a situation, a feeling, a process or something else helps to clarify the conclusion, situation, feeling, or process and can be understood and experienced by the participants.

In reverse, a topic can be broadened and opened up for new dialogue and new thoughts by drawing various possible interpretations, for instance, a company's role in the customer's life.

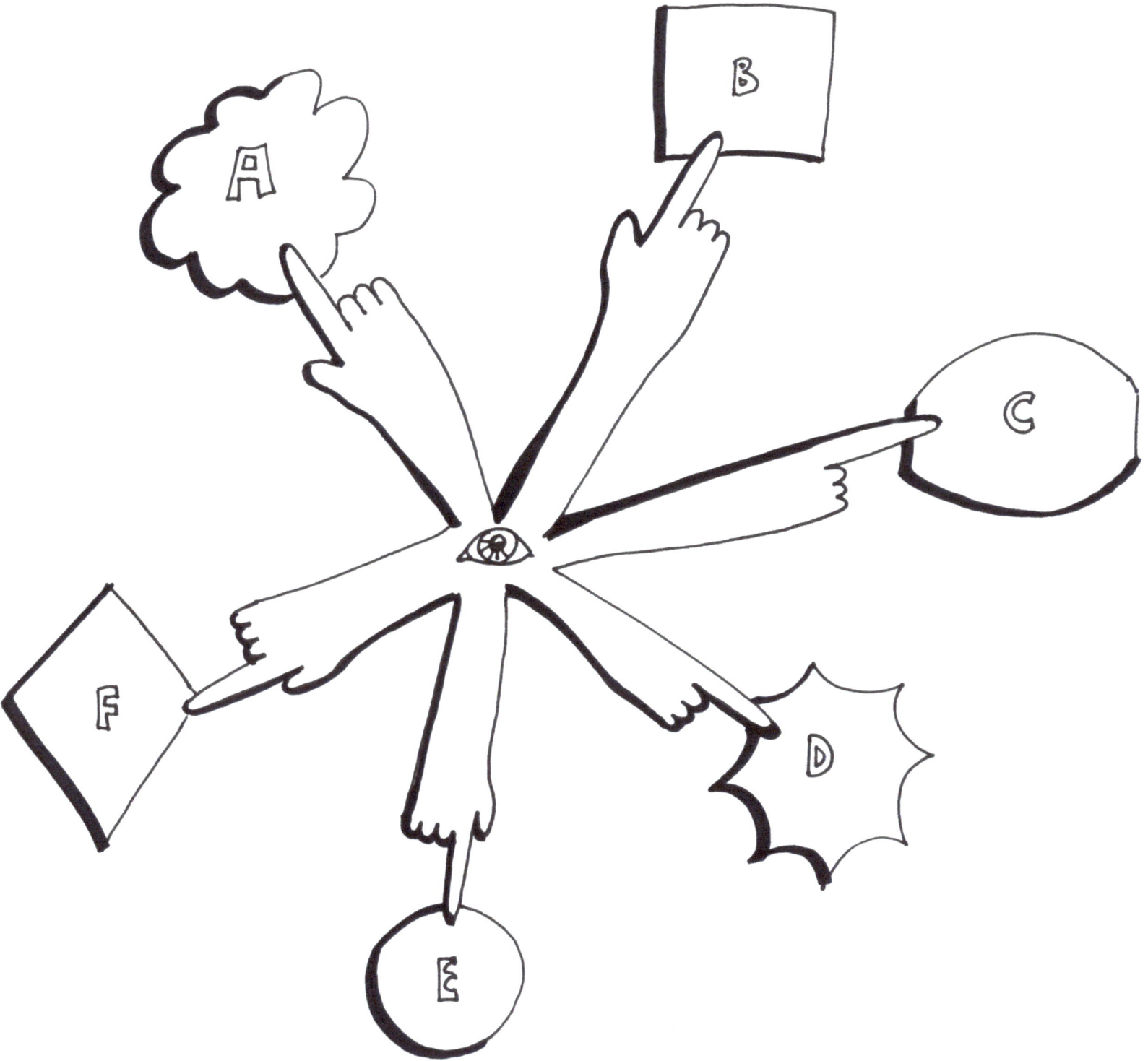

selection

If, for example, you are creating a vision board for your desired future, there is a selection process involved. Each time you put an idea on to paper, there is another idea you decided not to put there.

The selection forces you to focus on the right parts at the right time and can help you put less important tasks or issues on pause.

stickiness

You paint a picture in the mind when you draw. Ideas, dreams, and visions stick and drawing them dramatically improve their survival rate and your continued pursuit.

Groups can develop a common picture of a desired culture, family or business goal, icons to define a shared identity or values that stick. You see it, you feel it, you believe in it, and you relate to it: you can easily act on it!

REAL LIFE

equality

When participants in a group are asked to do something none of them are particularly good at, status becomes irrelevant, and all become equal. It is great for building relationships if everyone feels out of their comfort zone!

Through visual presentation, our (lack of) capabilities become transparent, which makes us all imperfect. It, again, provides a mandate sometimes to fail. It also makes our different viewpoints and opinions equally valid.

...WE ARE IN THIS TOGETHER........ TRYING OUT SOMETHING NEW....

COMFORT ZONE

infinity

A drawing is never complete. It is flexible and organic. You can always add to it and change it.

No mental picture lasts forever.

Drawing allows us to build upon previous perceptions or decisions.

It inspires us to keep developing our thinking.

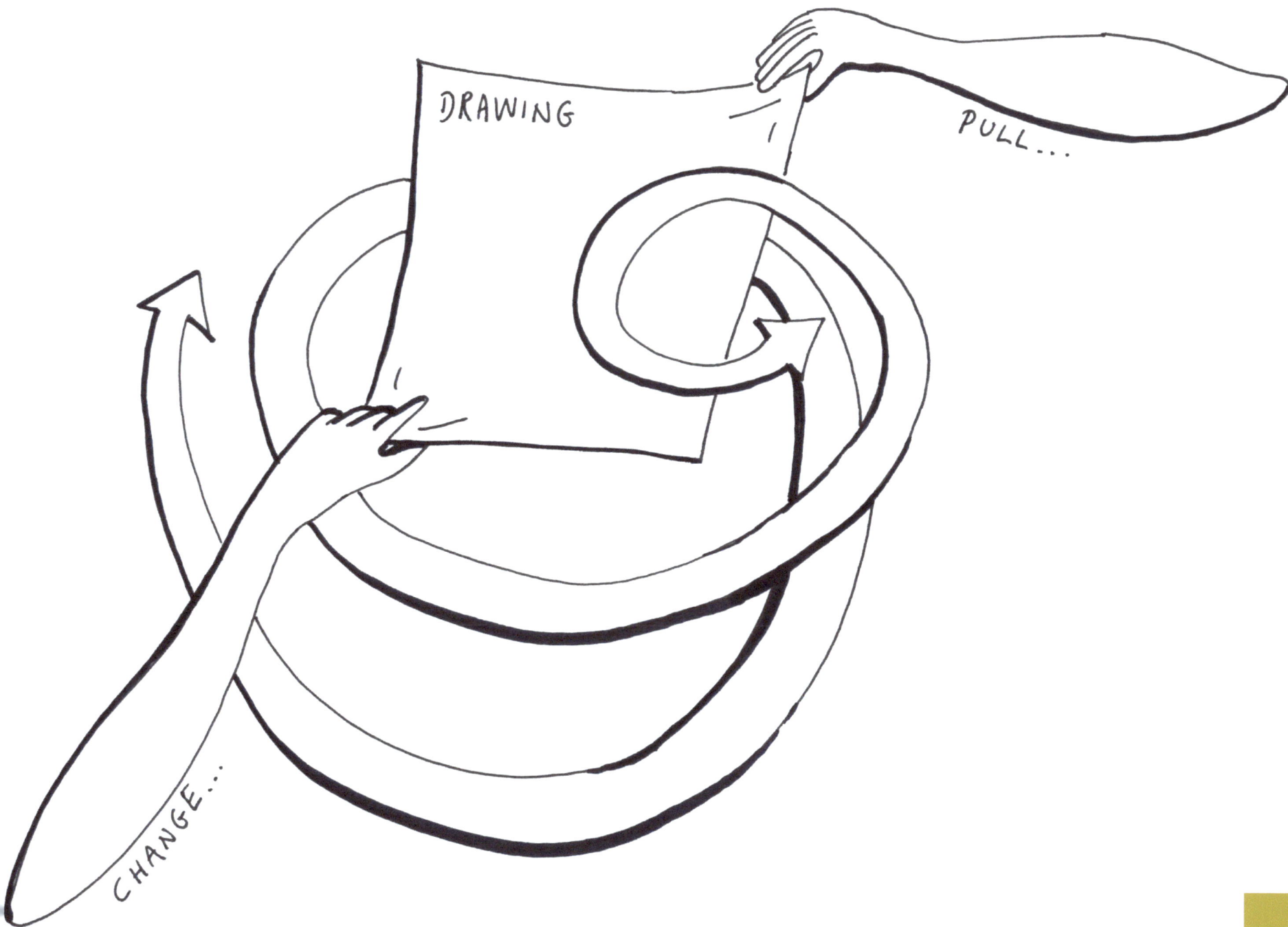

DRAWING

PULL...

CHANGE...

productivity

It is much faster to draw than to write. On top of that, the stuff you are dealing with is shown right in front of you for your brain to relate to and react on, fast.

You see a drawn structure of a project, you talk about it, make some adjustments, either alone or with colleagues, and the new or updated structure is right there for a new discussion and a new adjustment.

The clever thing is that drawings are not fixed, and changing them is easy and fast, which in the big picture, will speed up your processes and your productivity altogether.

problem-solving

Drawings initiate conversation at an abstract level as well as a specific level. It sets in motion whole brain activity, and because drawings are a kind of visual map of our imagination, they are impressive tools to facilitate the sharing of knowledge and eye-opening ideas.

Drawing can help us come up with better solutions and in a more collaborative manner.

relationships

People tend to create a certain connection between them when drawing. We see a different side of people, of our colleagues.

Drawing shows a sensitive side and allows us to get closer. It sharpens your attention and creates relevance and open dialogue. It invites you to be present and honest and to share. This is what great relationships are built upon.

become a
rockstar

graphic communicator

become
a rockstar

Apart from the primary outcomes of using graphic facilitation as a tool, you as a facilitator, presenter or documenter, are quite likely to obtain rockstar status in your organization. You will stick out as a creative and recognized individual, and your new skills will add significant value to your personal brand.

Most people consider it cool to be able to draw, and many are annoyed by the fact that they cannot draw or they *think* they cannot draw. You gain respect. You can express something quickly, easily, and in an intriguing way.

Graphic facilitation turns a meeting or a conference into something unique that people will remember for a long time. And when you were the person who provided that experience, you stick out in the market or in your organization.

Drawings strengthen our verbal communication skills. It is a platform to pick up important messages. Words are often poorly used and disappear from our minds quickly, but a drawing lives for a long time. Develop your brand by developing your personal communication and even personal drawing style.

drawing skills used
in 5 different roles

Your skills as a graphic facilitator can be used in many different ways. Once you decide to use visual tools in your communication, I recommend you first learn the most simple icons, templates, and guidelines.

You will get a sense of the infinite amount of possibilities, and you can begin to picture a plan for your work. As you go along, you will figure out which tools to use, when, and in what context.

You can go in many different directions after mastering the basics. As a teacher, I will ensure you learn all you need to take it to your own place and platform afterward.

Often people are unsure about how to use the tools they have acquired and the possibilities they bring until after the course. Ideas on how to make drawing part of your practice may arise or develop during the learning process.

You can begin with these 5 roles and methods: presentation, dialogue, teaching, recording, and facilitation.

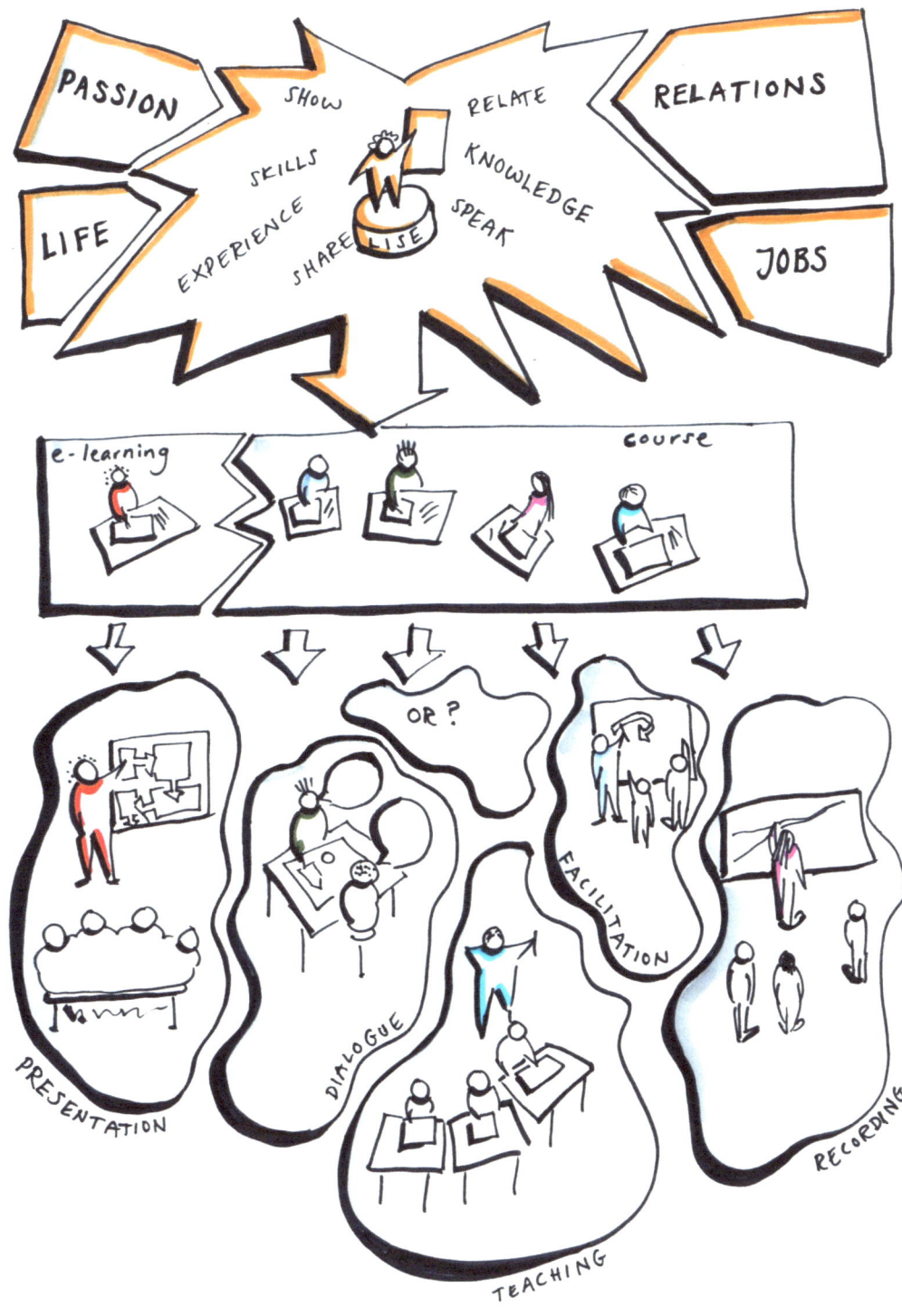

PASSION
SHOW
RELATE
RELATIONS
SKILLS
KNOWLEDGE
LIFE
EXPERIENCE
SHARE LISE
SPEAK
JOBS

e-learning
course

OR ?

PRESENTATION
DIALOGUE
TEACHING
FACILITATION
RECORDING

■ presentation

A presentation can, for example, be a poster that shows what you will discuss in a meeting or workshop – an agenda animated with icons and words. It can also be several posters that depict the topics for group work or themes for a plenum discussion.

A presentation is created before the meeting, so you present it as something fixed to the participants.

During the meeting, the presentation serves as a useful tool to help maintain focus in the right places and on the right subjects. It is a way to set up a clear frame that will tune people's mind into what is going on and when.

The presentation can be the company's vision displayed as a picture, making it easy for people to relate to, remember, and feel ownership for.

PRESENTATION

DIALOGUE

■ dialogue

You can use templates to set up a clear frame for dialogue, with a colleague or an employee, for instance.

The person sitting next to you will get a sense of recognition and openness as they learn that you are taking them by the hand, leading the dialogue in a clear and understandable way, with the template as a guide. What is being discussed stands out strongly and the template serves as a reliable and stable witness of your talk. After the session, you have the document as clear proof of what was said and agreed upon.

■ teaching

If you are already a teacher, you probably know what works and what does not work in your teaching.

Implementing the use of visual tools as a new way of communicating can make a huge difference in your role as a teacher.

With small adjustments, you can ensure students are moving in the right direction, knowing what is going on and why. In other words, you can make clear what you expect from them.

Devise a drawing or template showing the plan for a project. It could be a mountain, a bridge or another feature requiring participants to reflect on and discuss the tasks beforehand and commit to them.

You can then write or draw their comments and ideas on the special template. This will serve as a visual guidepost and mood board to navigate and make changes to as needed. With the template, the process is clear, and you can avoid misunderstandings and confusion.

TEACHING

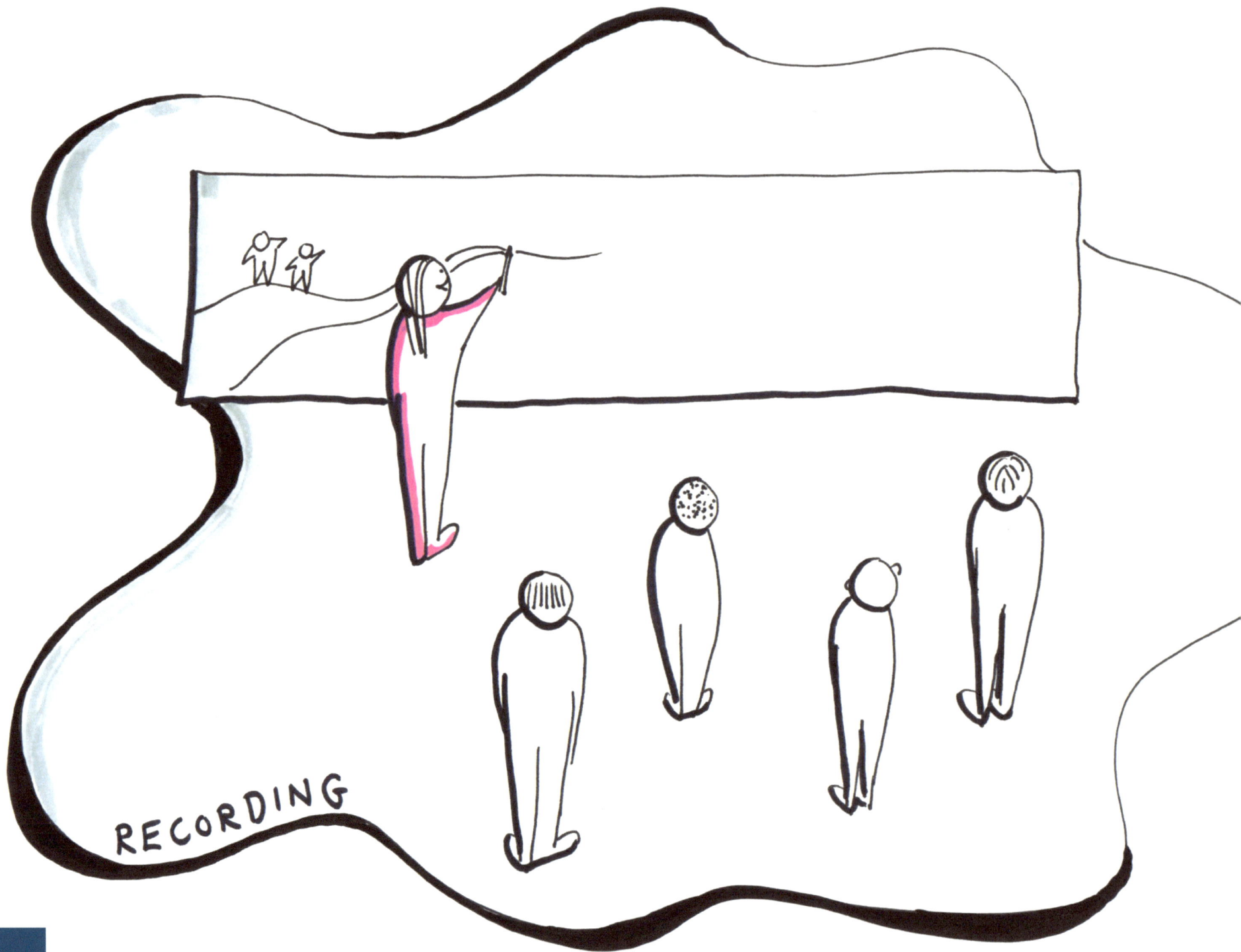

RECORDING

■ recording

As a graphic recorder, you complement the main facilitator – you are not in charge of the process.

Your role is to listen and grasp what is being said and at the same time sort out what are the keywords and what can be left out.

Knowing what to leave out in the drawing is just as important as knowing what to include.

In this role, make sure your client is familiar with your style before hiring you. Your client may already have an idea of what they like from previous experiences.

It is also important to emphasize that drawing is like handwriting: you cannot draw with someone else's type of line.

■ facilitating

In facilitation, you are responsible for the actual process and the expected result that is supposed to derive from that process. Your involvement in the content is much greater.

It is up to you to find your own way and determine what works for you and in which kind of situations. Are you on stage or behind the scenes? Are you presenting something or are you receiving something from the audience?

You can use your drawing skills in several roles. You could be an internal facilitator in your own company, an internal consultant, operations manager, project manager, team member in a product development group, or something else entirely. No matter your role, you can choose to facilitate processes and dialogues, document meetings, or conduct presentations using drawing as a tool.

You can also be a full-time professional facilitator, doing it for a living as an external consultant, hired for different workshops or delivering presentations for companies to use during seminars and conferences, etc.

Or you can be a graphic facilitator in your private life, organizing a party, special event, or landscaping design, and so on.

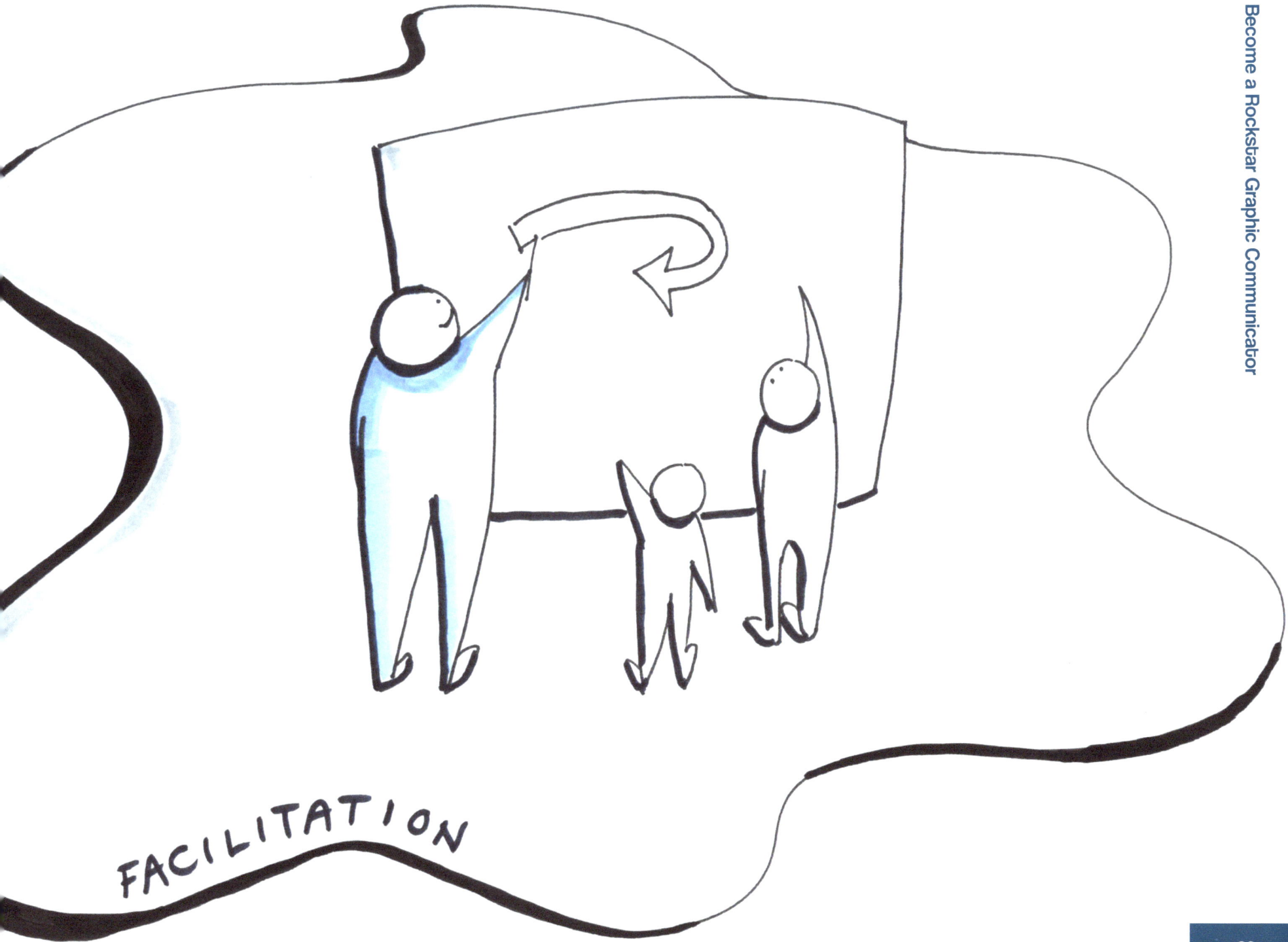

how to draw

draw

getting ready to draw

You are going to need drawing tools. You can start with less, but I recommend you purchase good quality tools. It will help you enjoy the process and produce better results. Although, essentially, what you need are pens and paper.

Select water-based pens, which last for a long time. However, it can be difficult to know from just looking at a pen whether it is long-lasting or not. I recommend buying Neuland workshop pens from the webshop Future Factor: www.futurefactor.dk.

These pens have a thick end, which is perfect for graphical drawings. If the pens are too thin, it is difficult to get the right focus and size the first time, and you might need to repeat the drawing, which is never easy.

You also need white-colored paper. In regards to quality, you want to look for a minimum of 80 grams.

Drawing in smaller formats is very different

from drawing in larger formats. You will need both A3 and A4 paper sizes. For workshop facilitation, meeting documentation and graphical recordings, you also need a roll of paper.

Make sure you bring plenty of paper for the job you are hired to do, and always assure your client that they don't need to think of anything but a nice flat wall, and you'll bring the rest.

When you start practicing, find a nice place to sit with good light (preferably daylight), enough space, and a pleasant atmosphere. It does not have to be neat; a little chaos with paper and pens everywhere enhances the feeling of being creative.

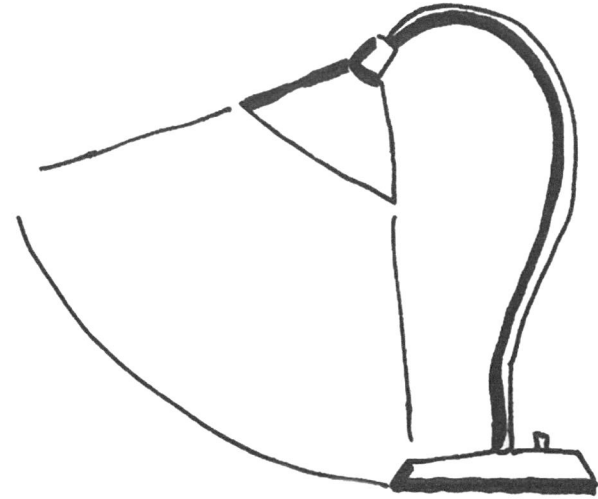

3 graphics frameworks

To learn how to draw, you must master a number of icons. To utilize your drawing skills as a graphic recorder or facilitator and fuel the superpowers as mentioned, you must learn to properly structure and explain concepts for a thorough overview of complex dialogues.

I use three basic frameworks to create compositions that serve different purposes easily.

1. Visual presentation
2. Visual templates
3. Visual notes

The visual presentation is a one-way street. The presenter prepares and communicates a message visually, i.e., agendas and posters. They provide a message.

Like the visual presentation, visual templates are also prepared beforehand but are not complete and invite dialogue. They provide a structure.

Visual notes are created during the sessions and do not require any fixed structure or content.

1:ONE-WAY STREET

2:STRUCTURE

3: OPEN NOTES

visual
presentation

Agendas

Before a workshop, conference or meeting, you might want to draw the agenda in a visual way. Ahead of the meeting, provide visual documentation of what is going to happen during the day.

This is a great starting point. You can easily draw boxes, and inside the boxes, you can draw or write what will happen at this point of the meeting. Connect the boxes with arrows to make it easy to understand that first, this is going to happen, second, this is going to happen, etc.

During the day, everyone can see from the drawing the progress that has been made and what is going to happen next. These are very easy points to collect from your participants. Add one or two small color elements, and you are a star.

WELCOME

Templates... (open)

Presentations... (fixed)

Visual Notes...

ICONS

MY DAY....

Guidelines:

DRAW WORDS

TEMPLATES

DRAW IT BIG!

DRAW A PROCESS

....STILL MY PROJECT....

PIT-STOP

MY PROJECT

LISTEN AND DRAW...

PRESENTATION

KEEP UP THE GOOD WORK! THANKS

posters

A visual presentation can also be a big poster made for a specific purpose, for example for a kick-off event.

Posters are a great way to show employees a company's goals and visions for the year ahead. Drawing adds clarity in itself, and if you use positive metaphors and signs that everyone can relate to, you contribute to better implementation results.

Hand out the poster in a smaller format for each person to take with them and put on the wall in the office or cafeteria as a reminder.

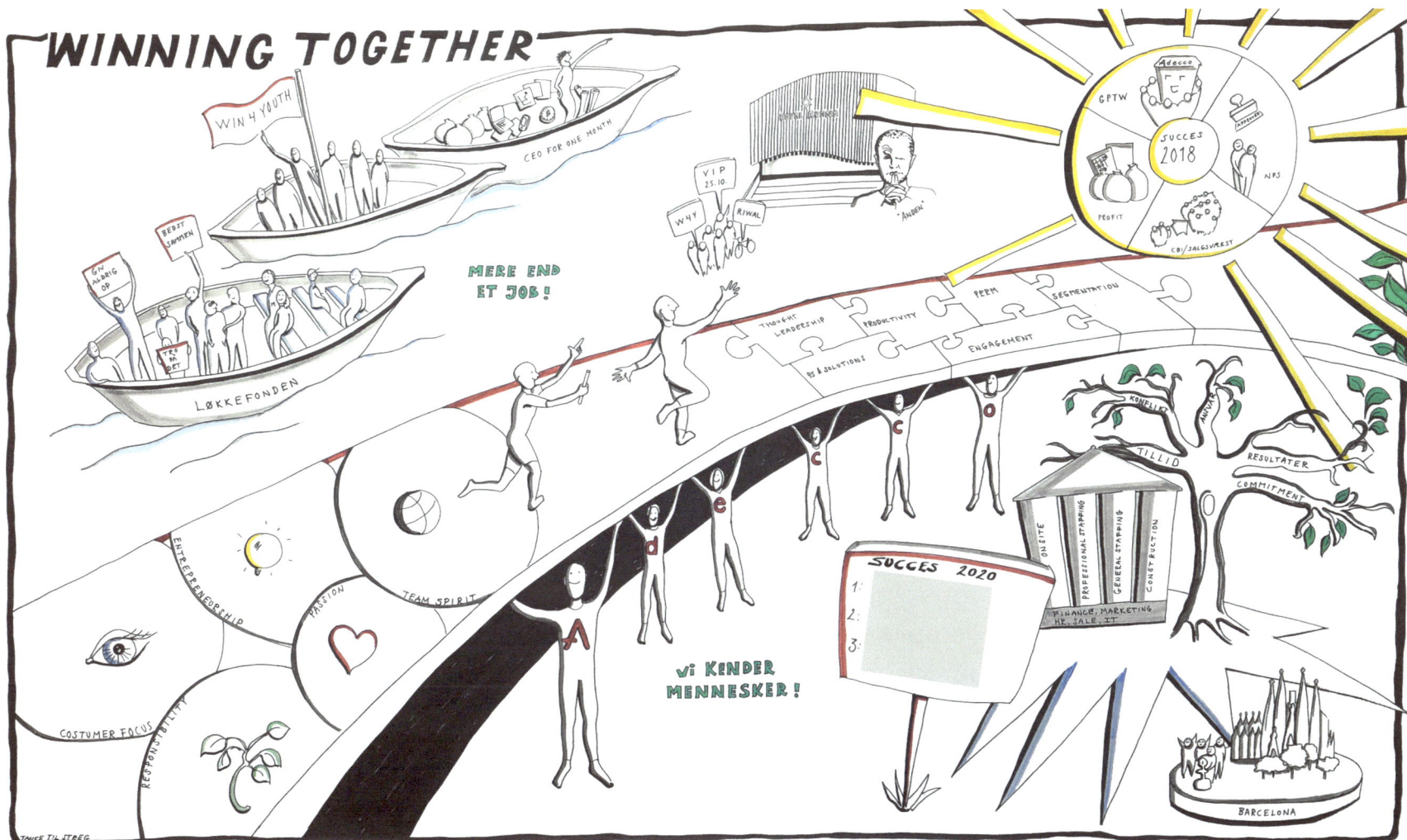

Illustration: A poster made for a company to display at their kick-off event with 150 employees

■ visual templates

A visual template is a drawing made beforehand. However, during live sessions, the template invites people to join in the discussion. You might want to ask specific questions with the template as a guiding frame to help you maintain focus and ask the right questions. This way, you gain the maximum output or information you need.

Visual templates can be used for project evaluations, project plans or as part of a strategy development session. It is an open invitation inside a fixed framing.

The important thing when using templates is to keep in mind who it is for, what you need from the audience or participants, what is the theme, and how you expect it to evolve in the process.

You might consider having alternative templates if it turns out that the template is too fixed or does not invite the kind of dialogue you had expected in the first place.

You can start by copying these templates and later make your own templates to better fit your purpose as you become more experienced.

IDEA GENERATION

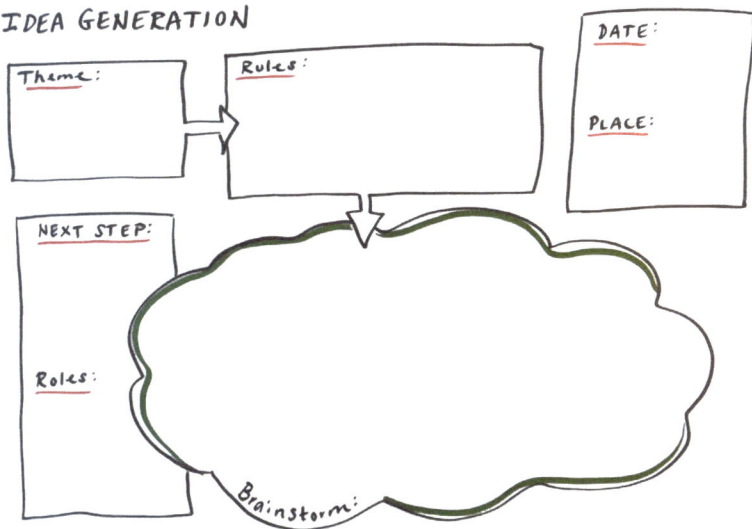

Theme:

Rules:

DATE:

PLACE:

NEXT STEP:

Roles:

Brainstorm:

PROCESS PLAN

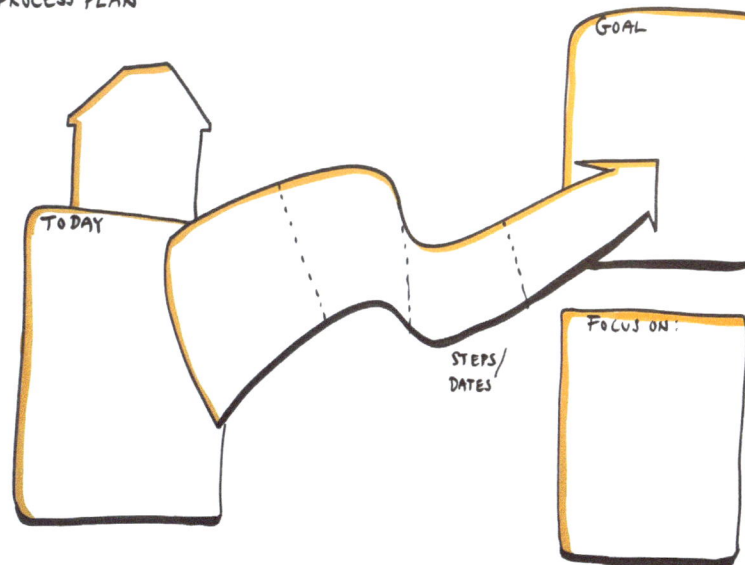

GOAL

TODAY

STEPS/ DATES

FOCUS ON:

EVALUATION

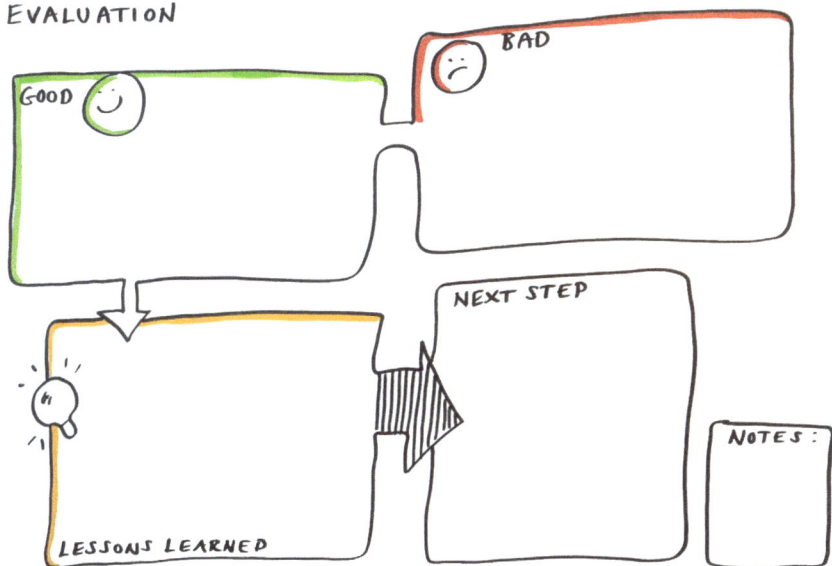

GOOD

BAD

NEXT STEP

LESSONS LEARNED

NOTES:

PROJECT PLAN

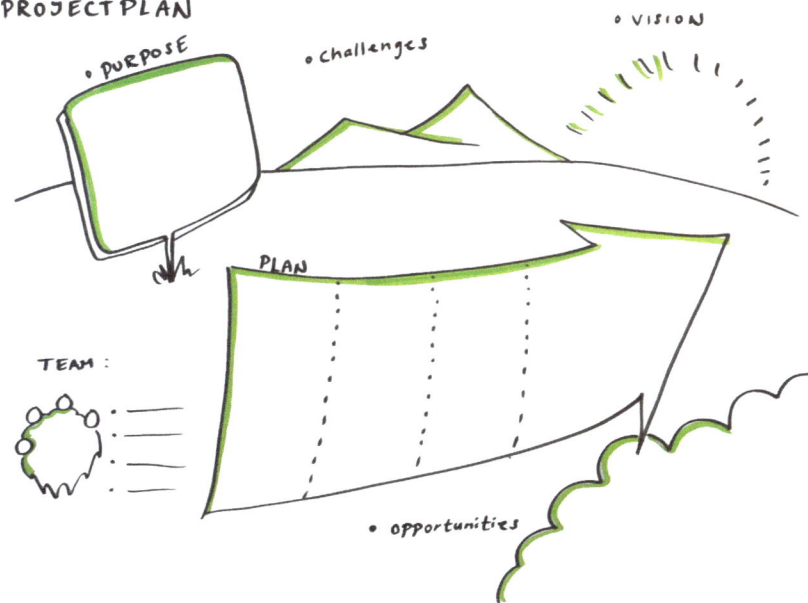

• PURPOSE

• challenges

• VISION

PLAN

TEAM :

• opportunities

MEETING

• PURPOSE

• AGENDA

Contents | Process | decisions

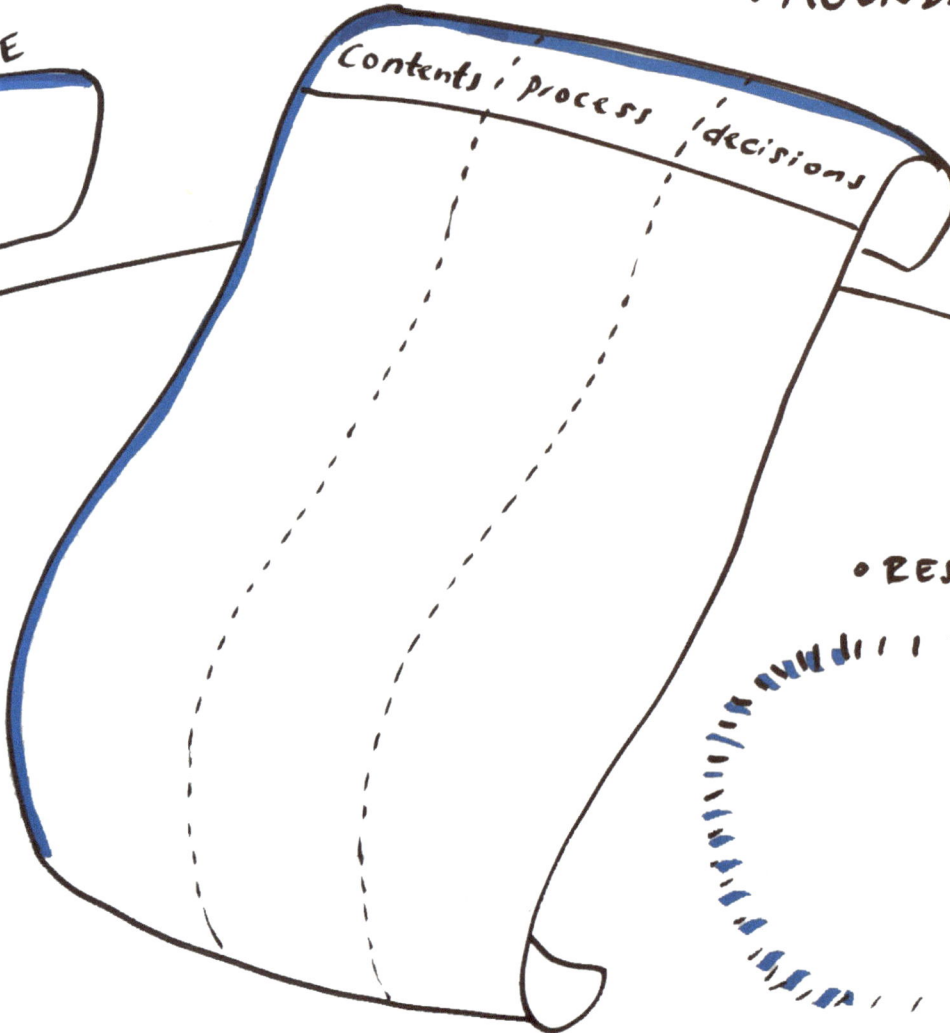

• Team

• RESULT WE WANT...

HOW TO SOLVE?....

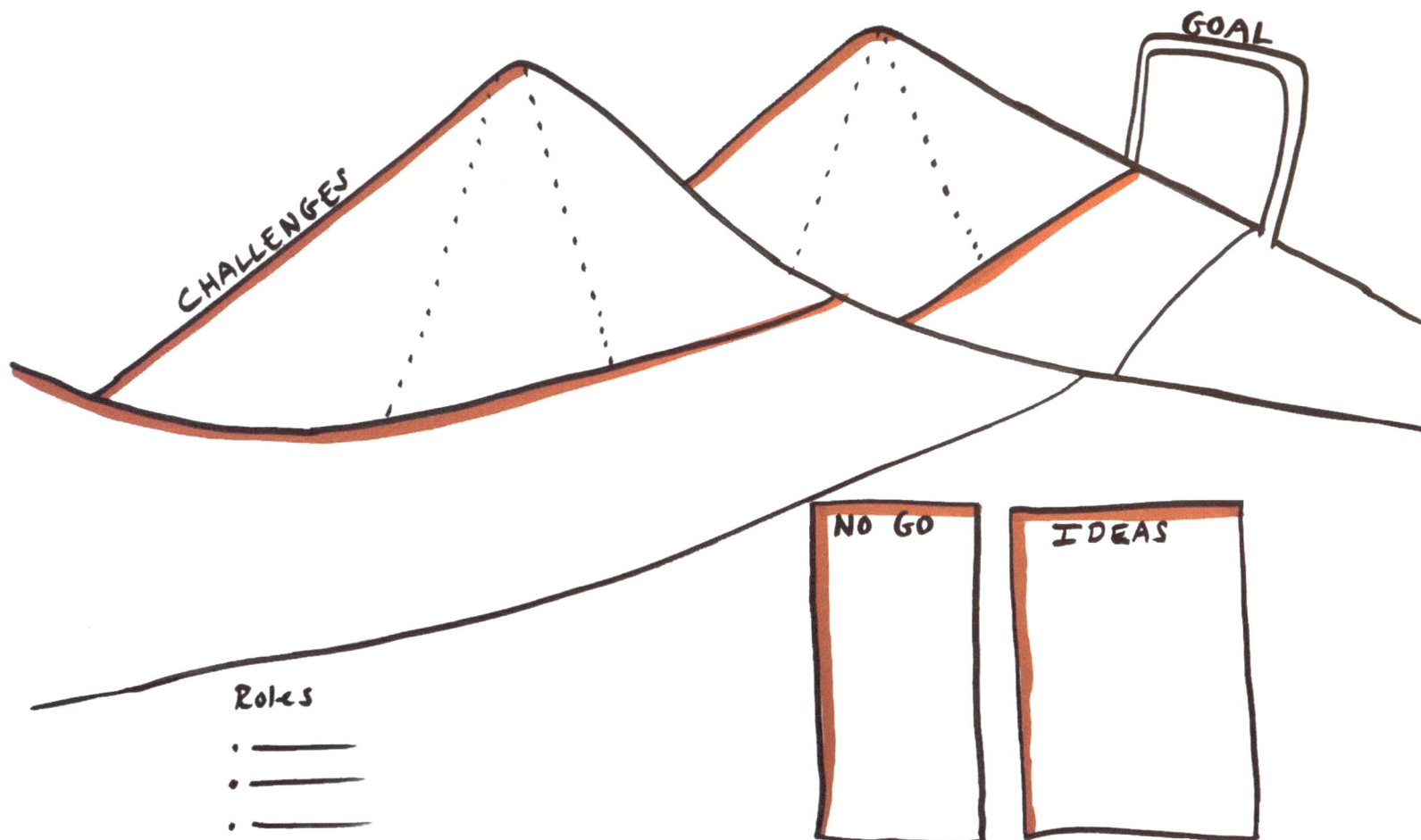

GOAL

CHALLENGES

Roles
: ———
: ———
: ———

NO GO

IDEAS

■ visual notes

Visual notes are drawn in a live meeting. All you need to do is put up a piece of paper, listen, and draw simultaneously.

You draw what is being said, you draw the points made, you draw whatever you think needs to be drawn – whatever makes sense to draw. Make sure you leave out stuff you don't need. Too many icons and text tend to muddy the main messages!

Visual notes are a powerful tool because it is made right there while the participants are processing their knowledge, opinions, conclusions or agreements. People understand that the visual manifestation is important; it has relevance, and they can relate to it.

At the end of the meeting, you might talk your way through the drawing, highlighting the most important elements and expressing what you have heard, seen, and noticed.

I often experience that the participants have ideas, comments, and thoughts they did not really want to share beforehand. However, the drawing incites conversation in a powerful way and invites participants to be more open and share what's on their mind.

Alternatively, or as a way to practice, do some drawings in your notebook and share whatever you wish to and find relevant afterward, or for your own use and benefit only.

A graphical recording at a conference about a future leader

A graphical recording for a Doctor of Philosophy (Ph.D.) during a speech she did for a small group of leaders

A graphical recording done for an internal employee day at a company

A graphical recording being used to wrap up a debate on "folkemødet" at Bornholm

A graphical recording done at a seminar on the topic "designing learning"

master 7 groups of icons

In my courses, people are often surprised that drawing is not as hard as you think. With a selection of simple icons, you can illustrate and communicate almost anything, combining them in different ways.

In this section, you will learn 7 groups of icons that will quickly get you off the ground and enable you to create amazing drawings.

1. People

2. People in context

3. Places

4. Transportation

5. Things

6. Arrows

7. Meeting or workshop activity

■ people

One of the easiest types of persons to draw is the star person. Start from the neck down and follow the steps as shown.

Illustration: How to draw the star person

Different states of mind, feelings, and situations are easily expressed by adding small variations to this star person, for instance, raising the arms or the legs, or creating different facial expressions.

Illustration: Variations of star man showing moods

There are many ways to draw a person. Little by little, you will find your own style. An alternative to the star person is a one-line person.

You can illustrate that the person is a child in different ways too, for instance, by drawing a bigger head or creating distance between the eyes. You can also play with the height and draw a smaller person than the one next to it, or draw a little person holding hands with a big person.

You can achieve a more profound impact by adding feelings or physical state. This could include morning hair, a look of surprise, exhaustion, or advanced age. Don't hesitate to exaggerate! If you want to highlight specific features, it is an easy and impactful way of doing it – and it is fun to look at.

people put into context

Groups of people can be illustrated in various manners, for instance, by simply drawing a circle for each head, an arm on each side, and some legs.

Don't worry about how many legs go with how many heads. Abstract drawings are easy to understand and too many details steal the attention.

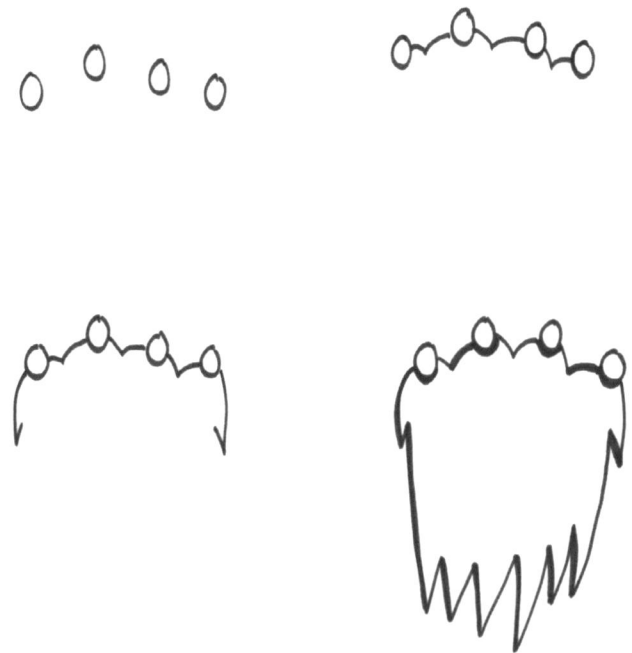

Illustration: A group of people

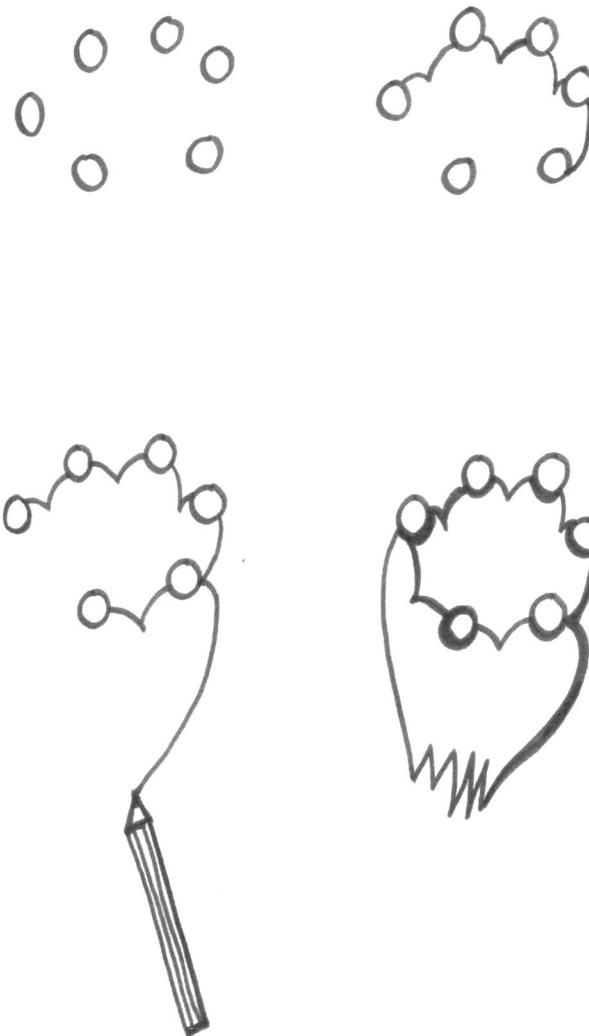

You can also illustrate networks of people or relationships between people: are they close or distant, are they holding hands, do they make eye contact, are they whispering or yelling, smiling or crying?

Illustration: People standing in a circle

people put into context

To explain what kind of person you are drawing, you can place the person on a platform and add words. Is it the boss, an employee or somebody else?

You can place each person on separate platforms and add lines between the platforms illustrating a network or group of colleagues.

Illustration: Add words to explain the role

Illustration: How to draw a platform

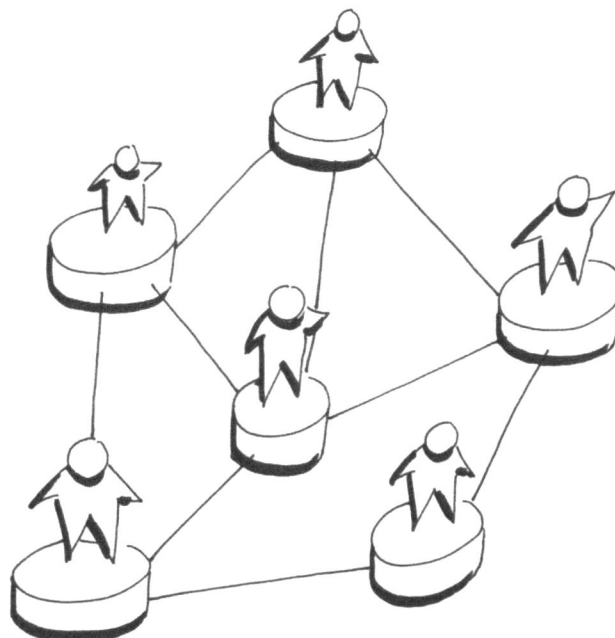

Illustration: Network, connections, colleagues

■ places

In your toolbox, you also need places: a house, an office, a shop, a factory, a city, a school, etc.

Decide if you want to depict the outside or inside. A home can be a house, or it can be a TV and a sofa. A factory can be a building with a chimney, or it can be an assembly line. An office can have tables, chairs, and computers.

You can find additional examples in the free workbook, accessible from the link at the beginning of the book.

Illustration: Buildings

The outdoors or nature can be expressed with skies, trees, lakes, beaches, and streets.

Illustration: Nature

transportation

You can draw all types of transportation from rockets, spaceships, and airplanes to cruise liners and boats to bicycles, buses, and cars.

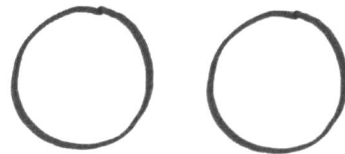

Illustration: Bicycle

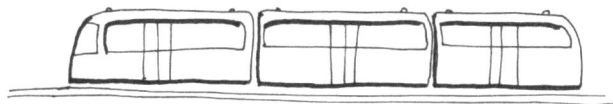

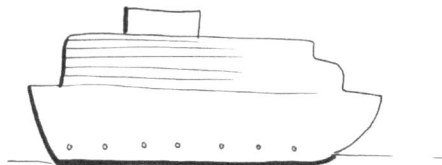

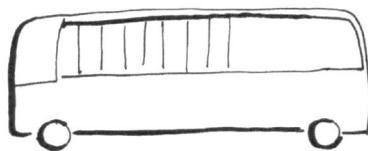

■ things

In your toolbox, you also want to have a few key objects like a book, a bag of money, clock, bed, chair, phone, and computer.

In a business context, a rolled up document is useful for illustrating a formal document or completed transaction.

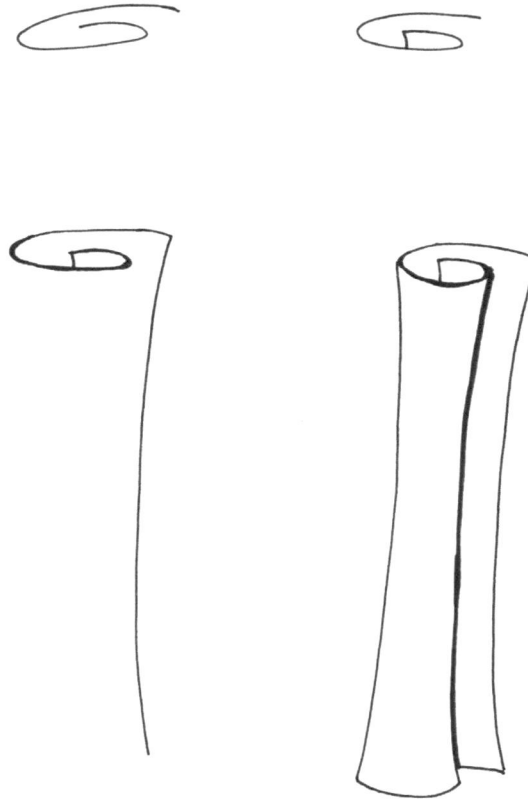

Get the free workbook with more than 50 items!

www.lisegrastrup.com/draw

To book Lise for a company drawing:

www.lisegrastrup.com/contact

lise grastrup

draw WORKBOOK

up your
game
with
professional
graphic
facilitation
skills

draw workbook

lise grastrup

FRAMES

SIGNS

ANIMALS

ARROWS

FACES

TEXT

COLORS

■ arrows

Arrows can show certain values or steps in a process. For instance, they can show a hard journey with bumps on the way, an iterative process, things going up and down in an organic way, or clearly defined steps.

Practice a selection of arrows and different ways of using them.

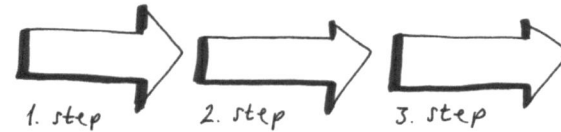

Illustration: Simple arrows

Arrows can also be used to illustrate a transition, movement or development.

Illustration: Transition arrows

■ binocular focus

Binocular focus can be shown in many different ways. For example, a finger pointing at a dot, an arrow pointing into the bullseye, or binoculars, glasses, or an eye focusing on something special.

FOCUS

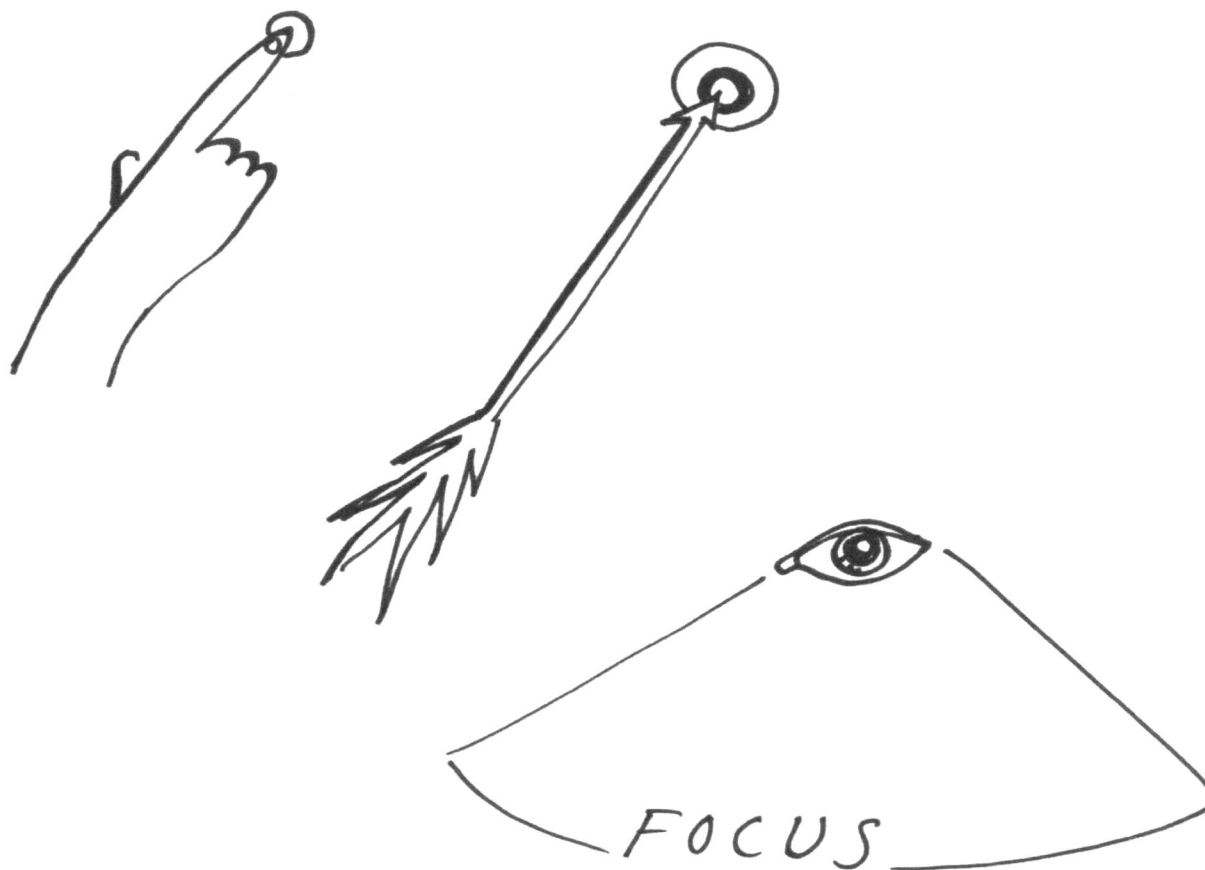

Arrows are some of the most important elements in graphic facilitation. In my online course, there is a whole section dedicated to this, which is too extensive to include all in this book.

The same goes for signs, banners and boxes – there are endless possibilities. Start with a few, and if you want to expand your repertoire, go to www.lisegrastrup.com/courses.

meeting or workshop activity

For your agendas, you might want to illustrate lunchtime or coffee breaks.

Speaking bubbles can illustrate dialogue, agreement, whispering, the elephant in the room, yelling, etc.

Create the person's profile. From there, you can work with the speaking bubbles and facial expressions.

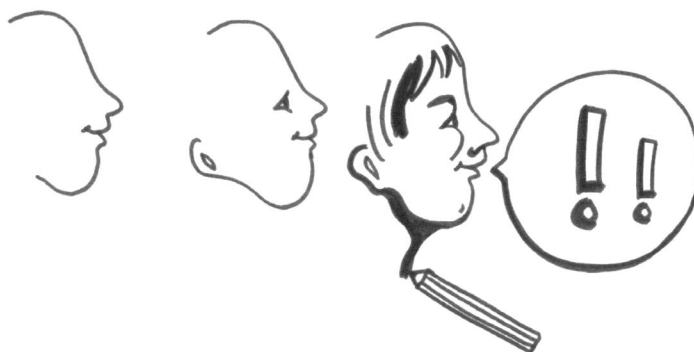

taking your drawing
drawing
next

to the
next level

guidelines

As a rule, you cannot do anything wrong. There is no such thing as a wrong drawing. However, there are guidelines you can follow to make sure your drawing will be orderly and tight and have the most powerful impact, allowing you to reach the hearts and minds of your audience.

There are 3 essential principles to be aware of:

1. Frames and composition
2. Create a good balance
3. Highlight important elements

GUIDELINES:

○ Frames / composition

○ Headlines

○ Body text

MEETING

○ BIG + small elements

○ Balance between TEXT &

○ Color codes – dark, light, shade

○ Bullets

○ White Space

PRACTICE AND HAVE FUN!!

frames and composition

You can choose one of two basic strategies. The first option is to start with a set plan. The second option is to proceed without a plan, let the creative juices flow, and discover what occurs.

In an unfixed process, the order may be more random, but in both cases, you should go through these steps:

1. Intent (document, enhance creativity, enhance agreement, etc.)
2. Outcome (what do I want to communicate)
3. Format (flow, priority, etc.)
4. Icons/components
5. Highlights and shading

For bigger drawings, divide your piece of paper into a fixed amount of parts, for example, nine parts. This way, you can put together a strong composition. Use post-its to note in each part what you imagine drawing. Move them around and work out a nice plan for yourself before you actually begin the final drawing.

This is a good way to structure your work from the start because the drawing will "talk to you," letting you know if you have too many or too few icons, bullets, words, etc. As you gain experience, it will not always be necessary to draw a sketch, since you will be able to visualize it inside your head.

Add a frame around your drawing to help the eye focus on a fixed area and know where to look. There are many ways to work with framing, and it does not have to be a straight line. It can be organic or anything you like.

Think of it as a theme. What kind of audience do you have, what kind of framing would be good or important to emphasize?

Also, add a headline to make it easy to understand what this is all about. Where are we? Who are we? Is it a meeting or a conference?

What kind of conference?

If you like, you can add body text underneath the headline, e.g., the date, place, and people present.

On the next page, you will find a drawing made during a workshop for the City of Copenhagen.

It shows how I work with headlines, colors, white space, and the kind of "unbroken line" that helps us read a drawing chronologically, which is an alternative way of using framing: the eye is guided to read the drawing and stay on track.

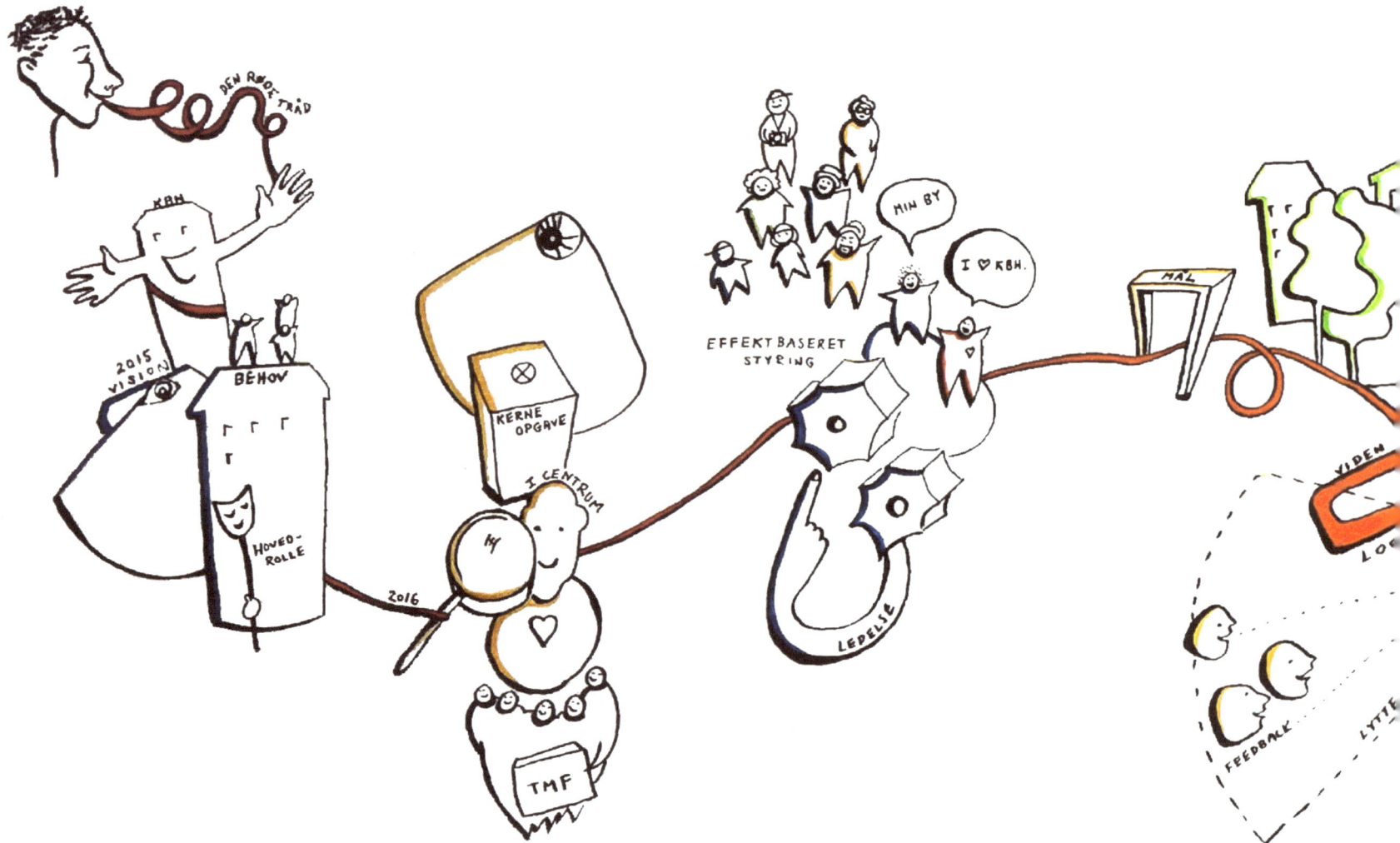

SAMMEN OM BYEN

FRA BYENS BEHOV OVER FÆLLESSKAB KBH OG KERNEOPGAVE

TANKE TIL STREG 15.12.2017

EFFEKTBASERET STYRING

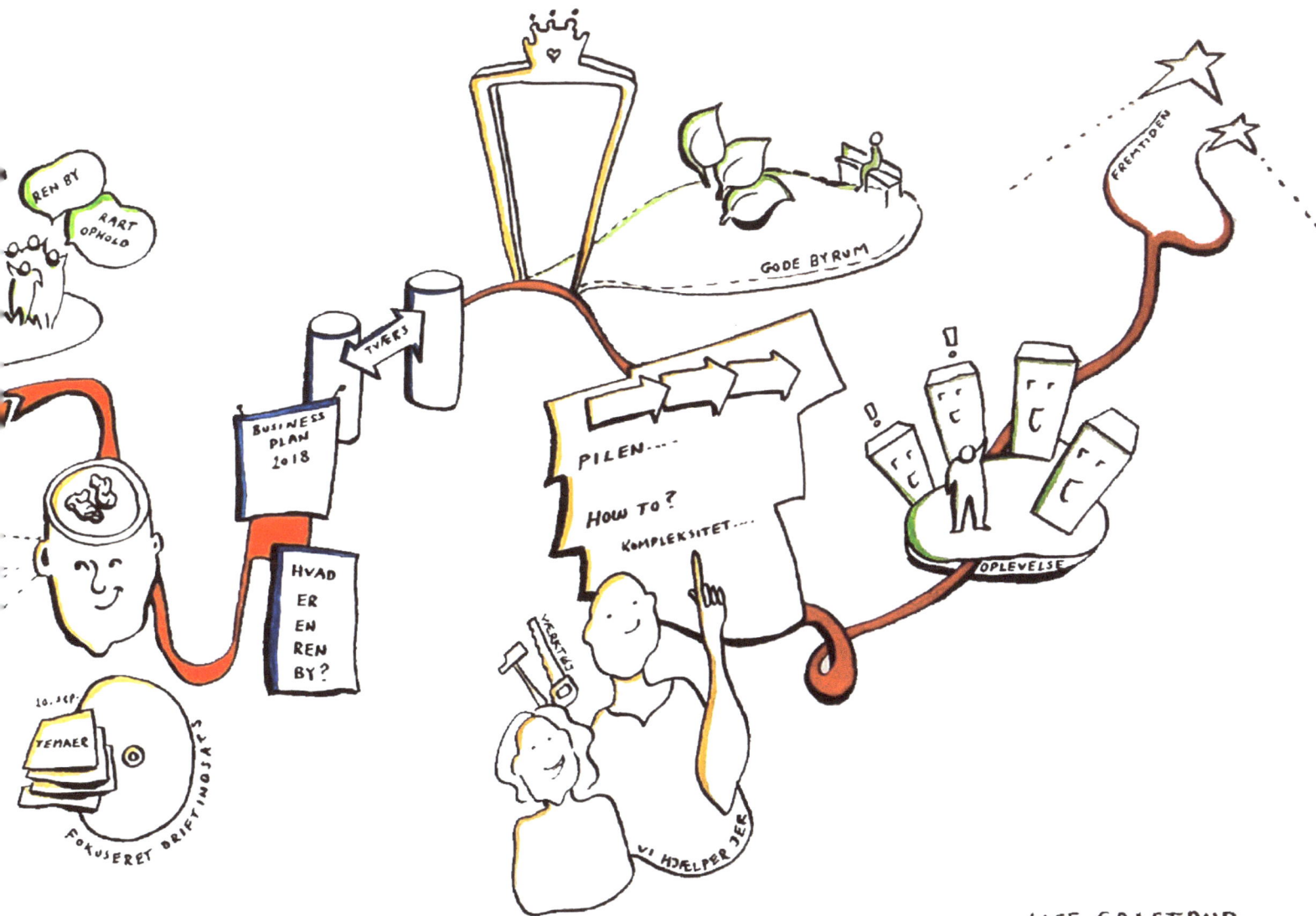

REN BY

RART OPHOLD

GODE BYRUM

FREMTIDEN

TVÆRS

BUSINESS PLAN 2018

PILEN....

HOW TO?

KOMPLEKSITET....

HVAD ER EN REN BY?

OPLEVELSE

10. SEP.

TEMAER

FOKUSERET DRIFTINDSATS

VÆRKTØJ

VI HJÆLPER JER

LISE GRASTRUP

create a good balance

Big and small elements

To make a drawing that is interesting to look at and present to an audience, you need to consider which icons to draw big and which to draw small.

Our eye likes the variation between big and small elements because the drawing becomes more dynamic to look at compared to a drawing where all the elements are more or less the same size.

If the number of big and small elements is equal, there will not be a good balance, which often comes as a surprise. So make sure to choose whether you present mostly small elements or mostly big elements.

I recommend that when talking about something of great importance you choose to draw it bigger than subjects of less importance.

text vs. icons

You must also ensure the text and icons are balanced. There must be more drawings than text. However, text is useful when emphasizing a subject or an important point next to an icon. Words tend to talk to us in a way that seems fixed and solid. This we can use when combining text and icons because the words you add become a statement. You can play with words as you would an instrument: is the statement ironic, serious, asking a question or pique your curiosity?

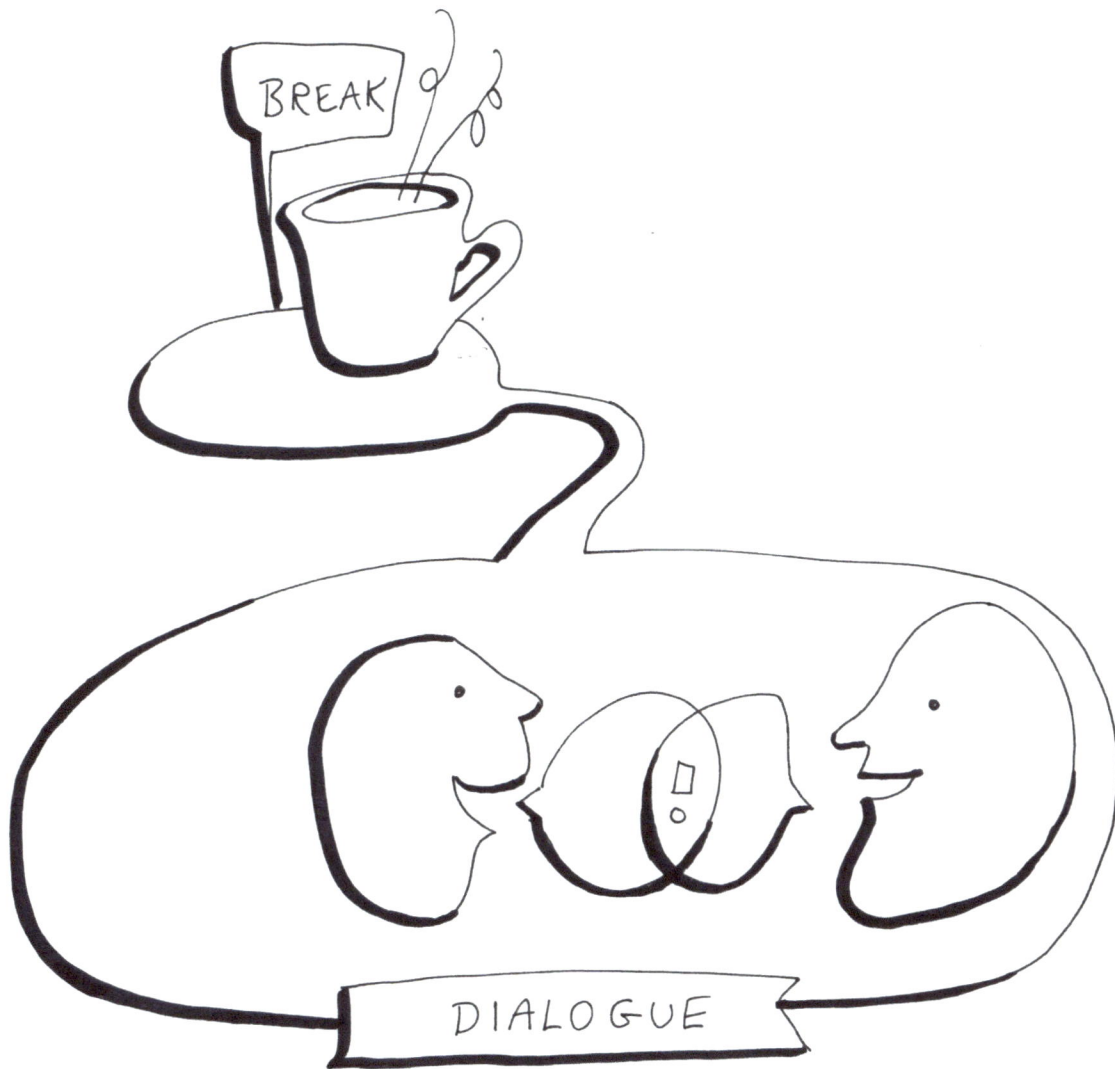

BREAK

DIALOGUE

■ highlight important elements

Colors

Colors can be used to highlight points and certain ideas because they demand attention and stand out from non-colored items in the drawing.

It is also important to understand our relationship with color is very personal. In some people's mind, a yellow color will be a bit over the top, and to others just perfect. A good rule of thumb is to think about your audience. What type of people are they?

If you are dealing with hardcore business people, cool, dark colors will be appealing to them. Accordingly, you might want to go easy on the very bright colors.

However, if you are dealing with people in the

business of teaching or social work, bright colors will most likely work well.

The elements you find most important can be highlighted by adding a shade or a color. Or you can choose to draw the important messages bigger than the less important messages. Make sure there is enough space available in your drawing to add some color. For example, make a double-lined arrow instead of a single-lined one.

Use colors to highlight important information or to group different parts into themes linking them together, visually.

Colors are a powerful add-on and must be used with caution. I recommend no more than 4-5 colors to make sure you don't mash it up and confuse the message. Colors are great but don't overdo it.

emphasize with shadows

Use both dark and light colors and add some shading. It emphasizes your elements. What you choose to shade has a bigger importance than what you choose not to shade.

Be sure you are consistent when shading in terms of which side of the page you add it to. The best way to add color is to add it at the bottom and at the left side of the figures to imitate a fictional sun shining from above.

Remember, shading can be done in any color. It does not have to be dark gray or black.

CORRECT

WRONG

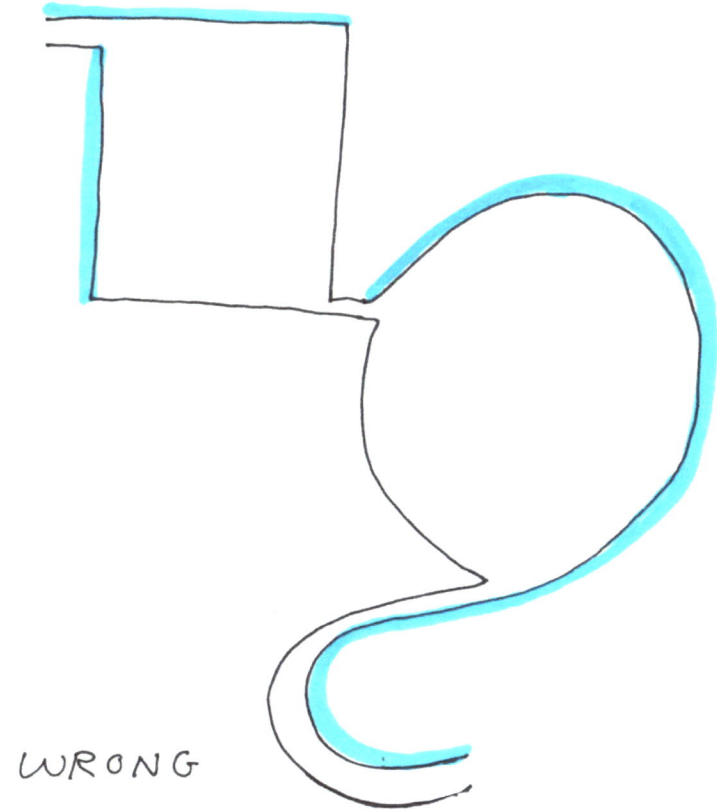

Illustration: Shadows used correctly vs. incorrectly

bullets and white space

Bullet points make your drawing easy to read. If you have written messages to convey, show them as bullets.

Our brain needs a pause between the icons and the text pieces. Make sure to add some white space, or put in another way: make sure to not put drawings, texts, and whatever else all over the paper. Leave white space. It makes it easier for our brain to read the drawing.

Illustration: A graphical recording using white space

more ideas for practicing

The first thing you need to do is to go through this book chronologically and practice all the icons. Then, you can progress to the more advanced section about composition, colors, frames, etc.

Don't postpone using your new skills in a live setting. Decide for a meeting this coming week, in which you will draw the agenda.

Or select a situation and purpose that fits you. Start practicing live, even if simply taking notes for yourself through drawing.

Move on to some more abstract illustrations and try to draw:

- Sense of belonging
- Celebration
- Soul

Practice wherever you can. Practice at home too. Listen to the radio and draw what you hear. Think about the points, the main message of what is being said, and what can be left out.

YouTube videos and TED talks are also great for practicing.

bringing your drawing

drawing

actio

into
action

courses and other teaching contexts

Graphic facilitation is effective in setting the frame for the topic, content, and timeline. It can provide structure and convey messages, which are highly relevant to teaching.

It sets people free and creates a learning environment where everyone is on equal ground. Graphic facilitation while teaching your best material is powerful.

You can, for example, use graphic facilitation to:

- Present a clear program or course flow

- Give a presentation or generate discussion using a template

- Conclude the most important learning points in each course module (you can provide these as a creative handout after the course, i.e., in a pdf.)

- Design a graphic diploma at the end of the course

- Evaluate the course

- Gather student testimonials

- Illustrate (or even animate) your marketing materials

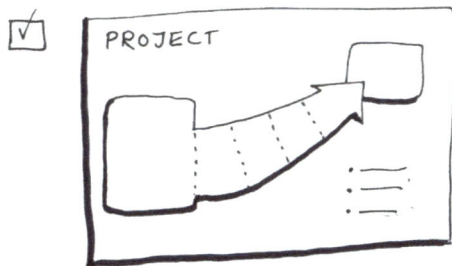

meetings, workshops and strategy days

Using graphic recording to document a meeting allows you to visualize what is said in real time and conclude with final documentation as agreed upon.

Everyone either agrees on the output or is forced to express disagreement. Graphic facilitation eliminates the "I didn't realize we concluded that" factor, which is common when meetings are documented after the meeting. Furthermore, the graphical recording reminds people of the various elements that did not get recorded during the day. The image serves as a memory board for each individual participant and the group as a whole. Each participant will remember more than what is depicted in the drawing.

They have either drawn it themselves on the spot, for everyone to see or you have drawn it for them, and they did not object. There is a different kind of commitment and clarity in making graphics documentation during meetings.

You take notes, make icons, collect knowledge, gather questions, draw questions and summarize the key points made in the meeting.

You can also illustrate the experience they were part of. If there is a group working together at a workshop, what did they discuss, how did they look? What fun happened?

You can build a kind of community within the workshop or the meeting or strategy day. Where are we going? Who are we? What is important to us? What do we need to focus on for the foreseeable future? What are our values?

This also goes for development processes, taking place over a longer period of time. Make sure you clarified your personal role in the process as well as how the drawings are going to be used. You need to know the direction in which you're heading, the people involved in the process, and the values to be emphasized, etc.

At conferences, seminars, and events, it is a mind-blowing way to document what is taking place. It is different, it is fresh, and it is clearly documented. People love it!

- Make a visual testimony of the most important points and activities
- Reflect on the people in the room and their moods
- Use it as a board that supports your summary of the day
- Create something to reflect upon during the breaks
- Physically attract the participants to take a look at and discuss your drawing
- Add humor
- Create a fixed point during the day
- Present the agenda up front
- Collect comments in a pre-made template
- Manage the time by using a pre-made template
- Identify the themes of the day
- Invite a certain focus in a discussion
- Emphasize points of view that can not be ignored

recorder

facilit

vs. **facilitator**

role 1:
facilitator

Let's take a look into the specific role of a graphic facilitator and the guidelines to follow to become a rockstar graphic facilitator.

First, you need to be aware, that you can't be a documenter and a facilitator at the same time. These are two different roles.

As a graphic facilitator, your job is to activate your team or group in order to make them part of a process. By using templates, you can guide the dialogue and identify the points and ideas. Asking questions is an important part of your job in this position – it is their project, not yours!

You must maintain a high degree of flexibility, and not be too fixed on how things should be, because it is likely that during the process wants and needs will develop differently than you expected from the beginning.

As a facilitator, you are in charge of the overall process, including the flow, type of assignments to be completed, maintenance of the energy level, need for breaks, snack time, etc.

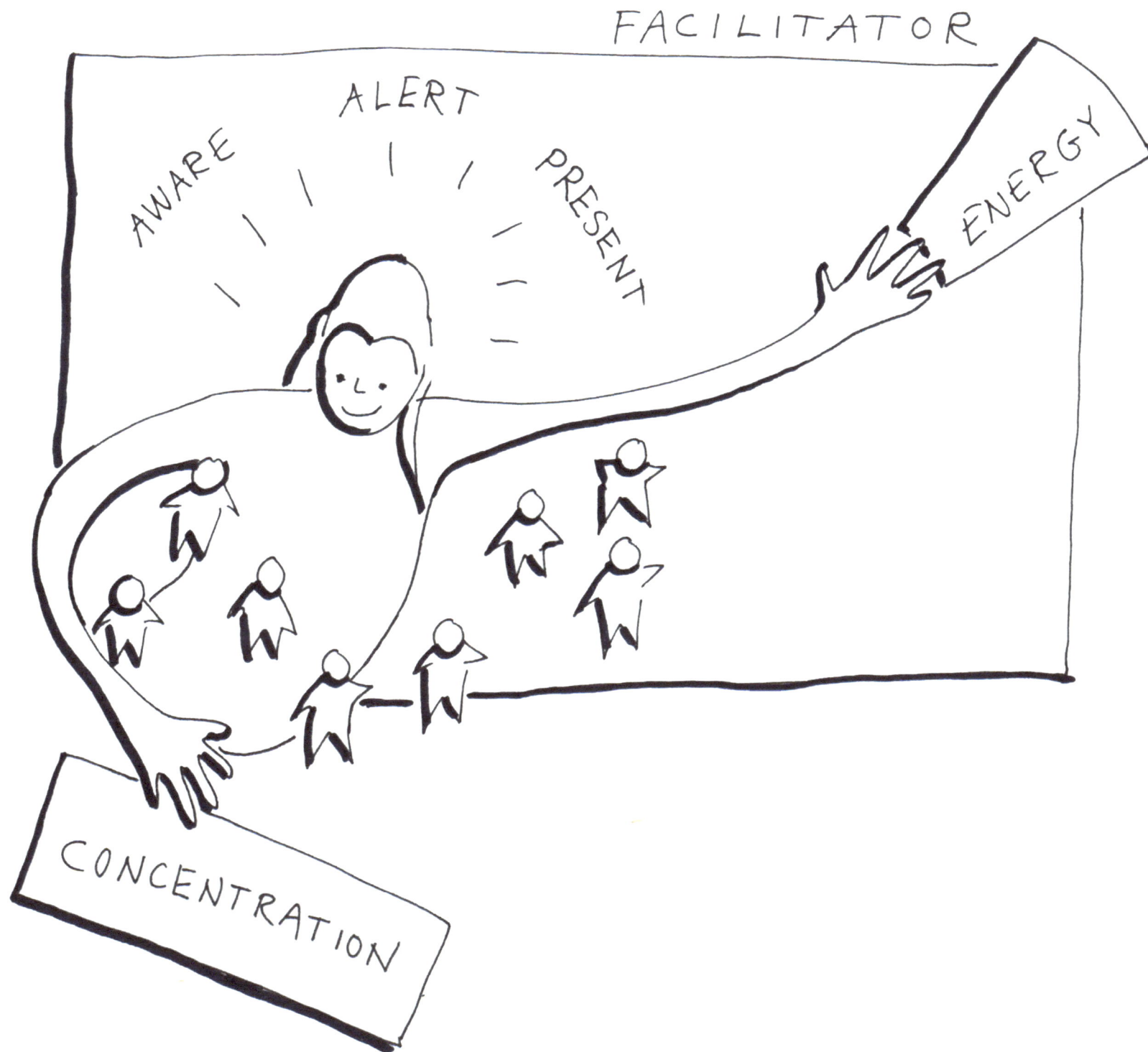

role 2: recorder

As a graphic recorder, your job is to listen and draw. You are not part of the overall process but might add your point of view a few times throughout the day or to wrap up at the end of the day.

Your role is more like a meta-viewer fixed on a specific theme, and you have the power to draw what you feel is important. You are in control and in the position to reveal elements that might seem hidden or difficult to talk about.

You can make this role semi-active by arranging a set-up with the facilitator where you're involved in the process, asking "So, what did you make of this, Lise, what did you draw?" And the participants can comment. Did the recorder get the point, or should anything look different, or should something be added?

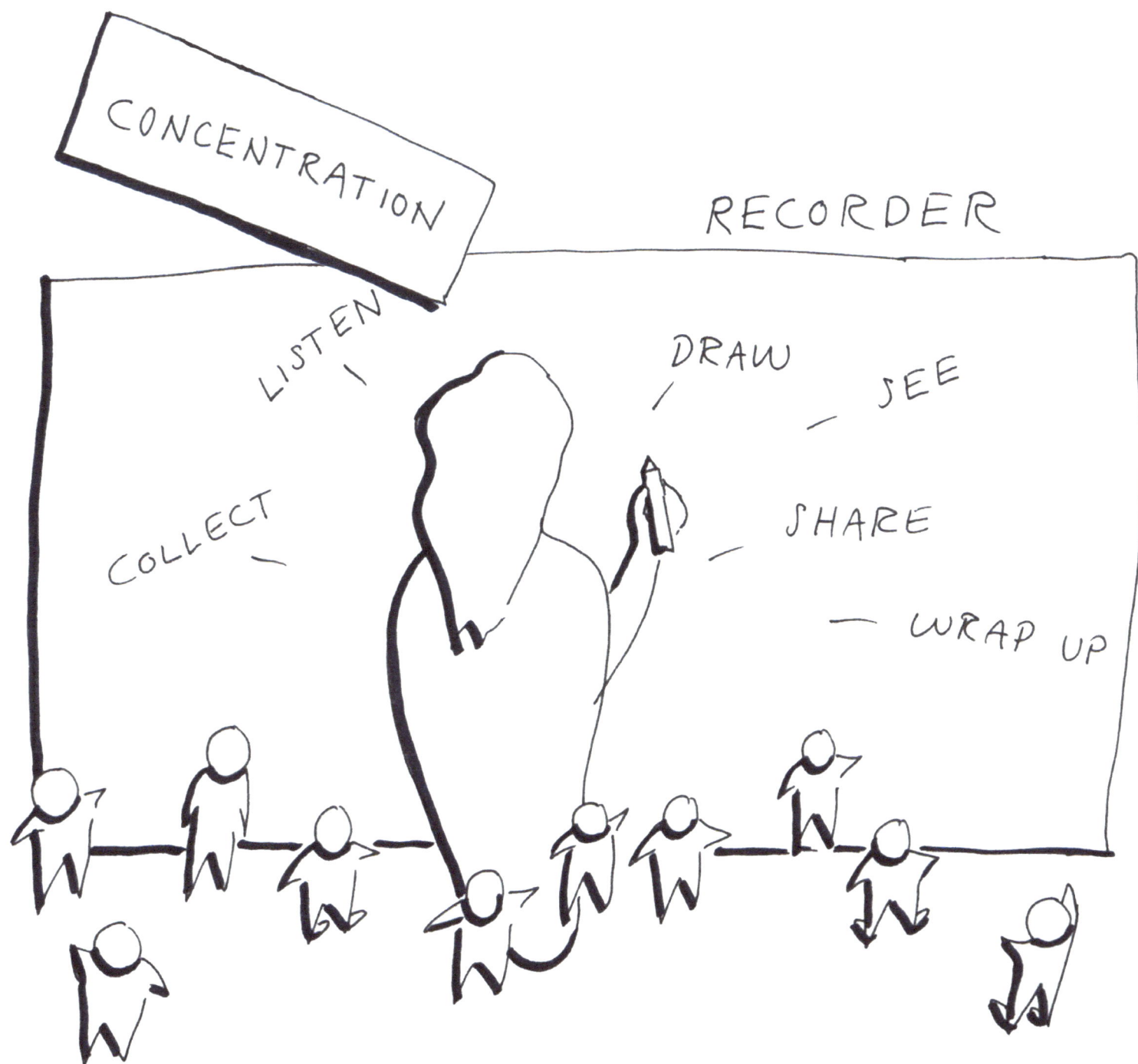

CONCENTRATION

RECORDER

LISTEN

DRAW

SEE

COLLECT

SHARE

WRAP UP

some useful tips
for you

You want your client to see that you are in control of the situation and they can be calm knowing you are a professional and will deliver. How exactly, you should act during the session depends on your personality, clients needs, purpose, etc.

To start, there are some questions you may ask yourself to determine what kind of facilitator you want to be in each situation.

Remember: nothing is fixed, and you can adapt the way you use the tools to each situation.

Ask yourself:

- How do I want to present myself as a facilitator?

- How do I want to appear in the room?

- What do I want to signalize?

- How do I want the participants to see me?

- How do I want to convey my messages?

- How do I make sure to engage them?

- Essentially, what kind of facilitator do I want to be?

You will most likely experience that cultures are different depending on the company you work with. And, of course, there is a difference between being an internal or external facilitator.

No matter what, you will have your own style, and need to work out the best way to communicate for each specific situation. If you are internal, you will be familiar with the company culture and therefore a step ahead. Use this advantage and see that the set up suits you and the people participating in the meeting or workshop.

An example: is it important to you that people turn off their phones and pay attention to the program?

You should make sure that plenty of breaks have been added to the agenda. You can start out by presenting the main guidelines or "rules." People will respect you for that. The same goes for other issues, such as starting on time and not 10 minutes late. Make it clear from the beginning what is going to happen, why, and when. Point out that there will be plenty of breaks, time to have a snack, and get some fresh air.

Maybe it is important to you to ask people why they are there and urge them to leave behind all other thoughts at the door and be in the moment.

Maybe you find it natural to ask the participants to say hello to the person next to them, to shake hands and to look them in the eyes.

Facilitation is about so many other things than the agenda. It is about the culture you create and the energy you show.

What you do indicates what you need and expect from people. The clearer you are, the easier it will be to engage people. Be specific in your communication when you present the exercises to the participants. They must know exactly what to do, with whom, for how long, and, not least, why!

At the same time, you must be flexible and feel what is needed during the day. If you don't read the signs in the crowd, it is tough to maintain the positive energy, and the more you focus on stubbornly sticking to your plan, the heavier the atmosphere will be. In the beginning, you may feel the need for a fixed plan. But with experience, it will become easier to adapt to the situation and workflow.

The combination of who you are as a person and the tools you choose to use forms the best version of you as a visual communicator and facilitator.

If you are hired as an external communicator and facilitator, you will not take the lead as much as an internal communicator and facilitator. However, you will be able to affect the way of doing things by doing your homework, assessing what kind of company it is, what is their culture, and what are their main goals.

If you are working as a recorder with a facilitator, the two of you can map out a plan beforehand, making sure the agenda and assignments fit the group well.

If you are hired to make a graphical recording and have little to no contact with the facilitator or program planner beforehand, you must come prepared and ready to listen carefully during the day.

The first few times, remember not to be too self-critical and trust the drawings will come to your mind along the way! Believe in your own abilities and take control over the drawing. You are the master creator!

3 tips to prepare like a pro

Make sure you have researched the company you are facilitating for on the internet, and understand who they are and what they do. What kind of visual signals do they send, what kind of style do they have, who, and how many people do they employ, etc.?

Print the list of speakers or/and participants. This way, you know who is there and how to spell their name correctly!

A stack of your business cards should be available when people come to chat and are perhaps interested in learning more about your work.

①

②

③

a word

model

on modesty

what might be holding you back?

Why do we always hear people say: "Oh, I cannot draw. I am terrible at drawing. I haven't done it in 20 years. I used to love to draw, as a kid I drew all the time. I had fun drawing, but no, I cannot do that anymore?"

Wise people have some valuable things to say on the subject, for instance, Brent Eviston, who says that images are the native language of the imagination. This is why most people don't dream in text!

People often assume that a good drawing is accurate from the start, but that is not the case at all. Drawing trains our minds to view our mistakes as part of the learning process.

Mistakes and imperfection ought to be seen as normal, temporary, and crucial to innovate and develop. New ideas only occur when we take risks, and drawing cultivates those ideas and leads to a natural way of finding solutions.

Sticking to words and numbers leaves gaps in our problem-solving skills. Drawing is a tool that allows us to tap into the world of new designs. Combined with language and mathematics, it offers a complete set of tools for solving challenges as well as communicating solutions to others.

However, a lot of people think they can't draw because they are not talented. But research shows that, as with any other skill, it is all about passion and practice. Drawing can be taught and learned.

Drawing is an active way of observing, analyzing, and recording the world around you. It's also a way of reimagining it. It makes sense to use visualization in development processes. The brain cannot tell the difference between dream and reality. By visualizing in detail how we wish things to be, we create new connections in the brain that would have been created by doing it for real. Therefore, it becomes easier to take steps in real life because the brain thinks we have already done it, and it realizes it is not so dangerous after all! Our brain remembers the future through pictures and remembers the past through experiences (K. Fredens, 2009).

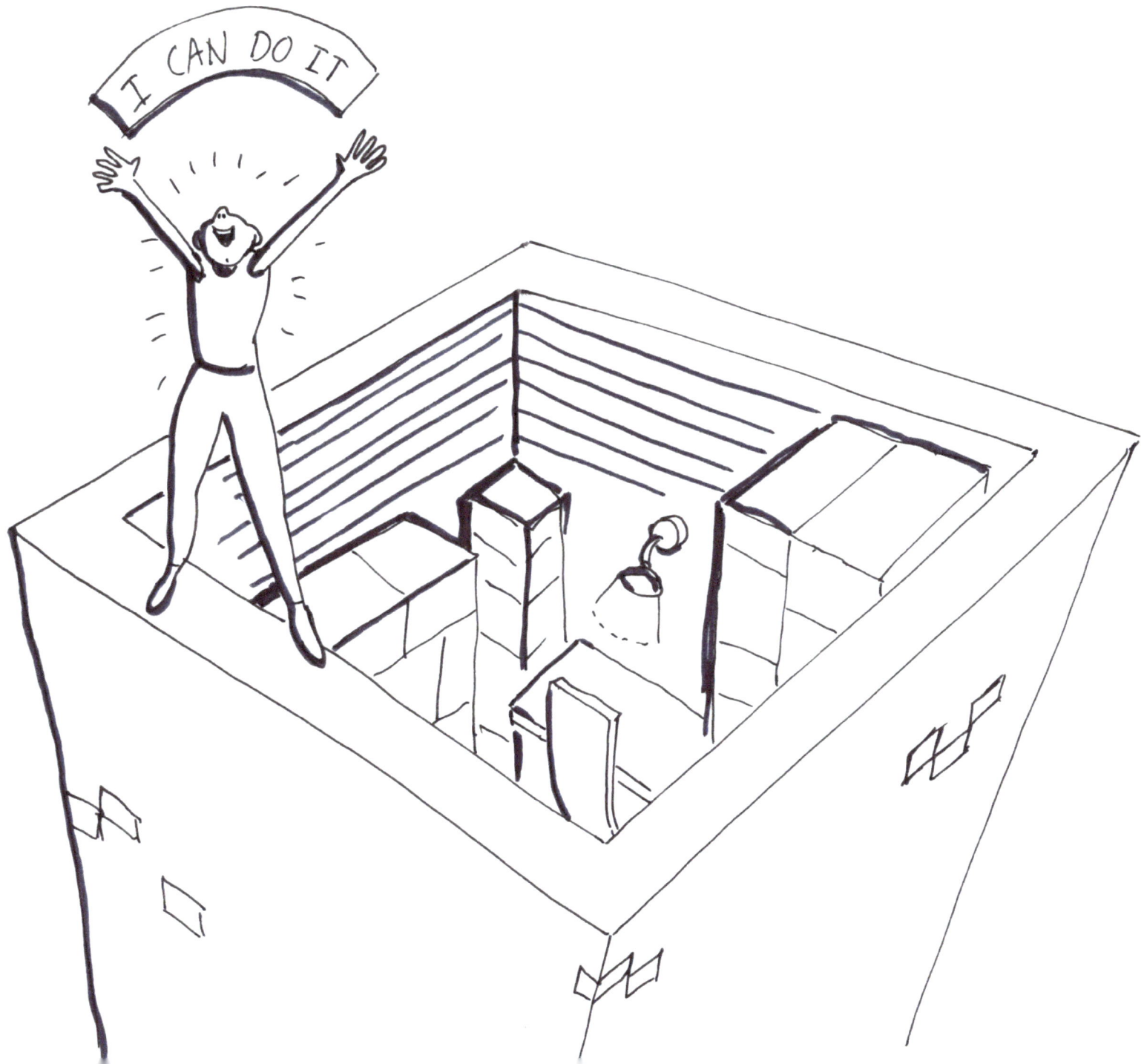

Graham Shaw states that believing we cannot draw really is a matter of belief rather than ability and talent. So when people say they cannot draw, that is just an illusion. All you need is an open mind and willingness to have a go! It is not about being the next Michelangelo, it is about expressing ourselves.

According to Patti Dobrowolski, drawing incites feelings of content and confidence; it helps create the life you want to live. Whatever is your desire, draw it! Once you picture your current state and your desired state, you can make the roadmap for change in your brain. When you see it, and feel it, and believe in it strongly, you will be able to act on it and make the changes you wish for. Your brain will find the right path and the right steps for you to take.

Furthermore, drawing and dreaming make your

brain excrete the happiness hormones serotonin and oxytocin. So drawing will make you feel happy and cool!

As Maya Angelou puts it: "A solitary fantasy can transform a million realities."

We all have a fear of not being good enough, not being accepted by the community, and being judged as "wrong." But by tricking our brain and getting past the center of fear (amygdala), we can achieve a lot, using drawings as a strong tool for understanding, development, and change.

This is why there is no reason, whatsoever, for holding back when it comes to drawing. You have so much to gain and nothing to lose. So what are you waiting for?

how to overcome

the
barrier

prettiness
is irrelevant

Here is some good news for you: You can actually learn to draw and quite easily. Don't be shy. Throw away your fear of failing, your fear of not being good enough. It is not about a pretty drawing, it is about communication.

I guarantee you can learn to draw again. You can learn how to do simple illustrations and have great results. Simplicity is desirable. Complexity is not. Prettiness is simply irrelevant.

Graphic facilitation is about communication. In my drawing course, I teach how to draw in a simple way: simple icons, templates, and how to make visual notes. I have never had someone in my course who couldn't learn the basics in a short time.

Another important thing: overload is ok in any learning process. It is ok if you get fed up and think, "This is difficult, I am not good enough, I am not a success in drawing." Don't worry, it is normal. Start with a small piece of paper and then a bigger piece of paper. Start doing shorter live sessions and then longer. Build your new skill over time, but appreciate that, though not perfect, you are contributing with something highly valuable already from the beginning. You will gain more courage along the way, and it is highly unlikely you won't find it super fun very quickly. All my students experience that they earn huge respect and admiration even with basic skills.

My courses are outlined with the encouragement to move forward. They maintain a certain pace. However, we do not want you to be overwhelmed, so there are tons of exercises and examples to practice in each step.

This does not mean you have to master all of them. It is to help you stay motivated and keep practicing without stopping too much to overthink things. It does not help to be a perfectionist.

Practice does not have perfection as a purpose. On the contrary, the purpose is to do it enough times to make you relax, take the imperfect in stride, and have fun.

People like to hear stories. Tell yours, we want to hear it. Share what you hear and how you experience what is going on in the room while facilitating. Take a pause whenever you want it, have a cup of coffee, and enjoy.

Nothing comes without practice. You have to practice. You must commit to it: "I want to practice this, and I want to become a rockstar graphic facilitator." But there is no rush, and there is no panic. Just get started. Then develop gradually along the way. Steal with pride. We do not own what we draw, so be inspired by what you see other people have drawn or search on

Google to brainstorm ideas.

Meet with other people, make a small group, do this together. It is much more fun when you share it. People in my courses quickly overcome any barriers and share their work. They love to discuss different interpretations and have a lot of fun when something is completely off or almost impossible to identify. Fail fast and fail forward. It's fun! And most importantly, even

these imperfect drawings represent an incredible opportunity to communicate and reach a deeper understanding of a feeling or subject.

Pretty illustrations or less pretty illustrations are equally excellent conversation starters! Therefore listening and interpreting are your key strengths – and most likely skills you already have. Learning to draw is simply adding to your superpowers!

"THANK YOU, Lise Grastrup. In just one day, Lise managed to open up my mind to the act of drawing. I never did draw because in my head there has always been a voice telling me I definitely couldn't do it. Now, I have the courage to do it and will even claim that I have mastered the art of drawing – and I will never stop!"

Carina Cederbye, CEO

"Thank you for a great course in graphic facilitation. I just used drawing in my presentation and it was so cool! The feedback I received from the participants was: 'That is so nice, can I keep it?' or 'That is going to hang on my wall' to 'It's so much better than PowerPoint.' I am pleased with the result myself, despite the imperfections."

Malene Keil Sørensen, Senior Consultant

"Incredible how much Lise Grastrup managed to teach us in just 7 hours. She was teaching a group of consultants in our company.

The program was very thought through, and the speed and the types of assignments made sure that we got the tools and instructions in the correct order to become confident with them.

First, we were introduced to the basic icons, then some templates and standard guidelines, and in the end, we were able to bring the tools into action and apply them to our own needs and context.

Already the day after the course, we used the new skills at an intern strategy day, which was very strong and powerful!"

Henrik Bogh, Marketing Manager

the DRAW

model

4 steps to nail graphic facilitation

Certain steps are crucial when you throw yourself into the art of communicating through drawings. This model I have developed is called DRAW and takes you through each step of the graphic facilitation process.

It is meant to guide you as far as it makes sense to you. You will find it useful as a kind of checklist whenever you are going to create a visual plan or piece for facilitation and communication.

DRAW 360°

RELATE

AID

DESIGN

WRAP UP

- PROBLEM
- ISSUE
- OR?

- VISION
- PROBLEM SOLVED
- OR?

step 1
design

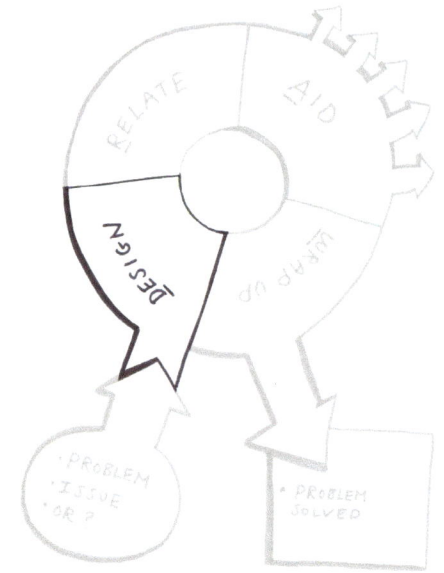

- How will you facilitate the process?

- Understand the why. What problem is the client looking to solve?

- Will you use a presentation, template or visual notes?

- What do you need to bring?

- Will you begin with a pre-drafted logo using a very light pencil to be fully drawn in pen at the event (setting the scene)?

- How many people will be present, what will be the size of the drawing, etc.?

step 2
relate

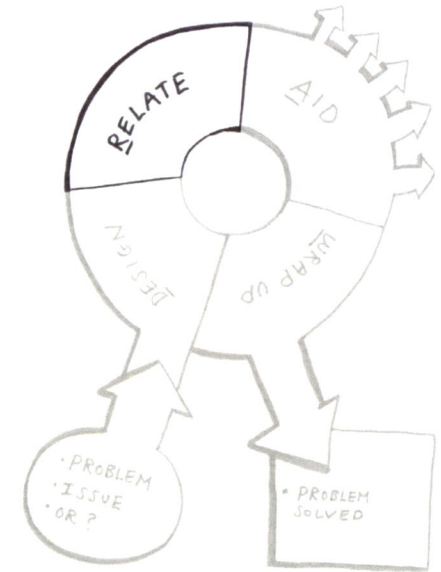

- Understand who are the participants.

- Create a relaxed and trusting atmosphere.

- Be aware of hidden agendas, fear, etc.

- Read body language.

- Make them fans.

- Make sure people are mentally and physically present.

step 3
aid

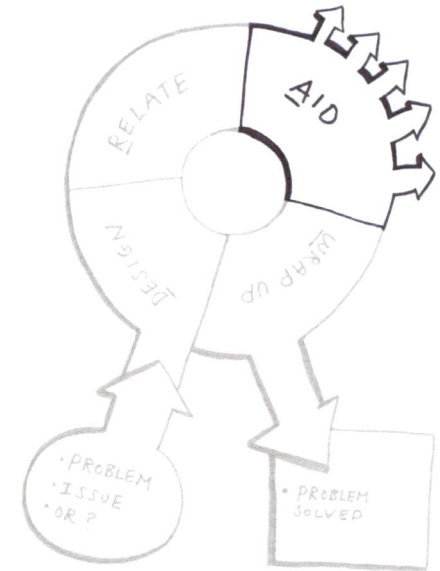

- Present a visual agenda to begin.

- You are there to help solve a problem.

- Ask questions, invite discussion, and summarize clearly.

- Identify how to cut out unnecessary information.

- Prioritize what you choose to draw.

- Build up the overall structure and flow.

- Transform complicated issues into simple forms and icons.

- Show the audience that you get the point and engage with them.

- Give them your best images spiced up with good humor.

- Address critics from the audience.

- Listen to the crowd and ask if they agree: did you miss something?

- Prove you are a professional – find a balance between being the artist on stage and the drawing pen with listening ears.

step 4
wrap up

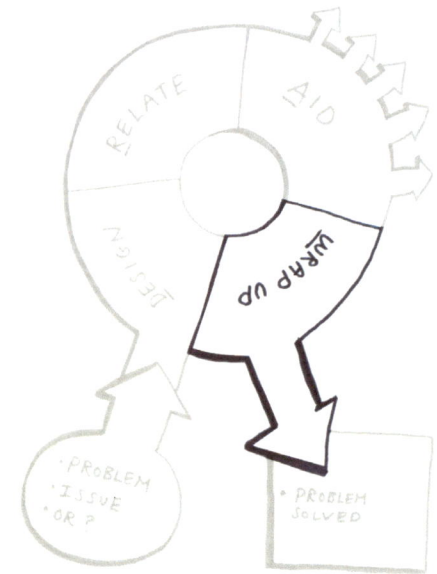

- Playback to the audience what you heard.

- Complete the drawing.

- Evaluate the session with the participants (for you to learn but mostly for giving them the opportunity to express how they feel about the result. This increases the actual value of the sessions because of the commitment involved in accepting the outcome).

- Is there some work to follow up on? Is there a need for additional drawings, or handouts taken from the recording or templates? Do you need to take photos of the material to send in an email afterword? Encourage participants to take the drawings to share with people who did not participate in the workshop, meeting, conference, etc.

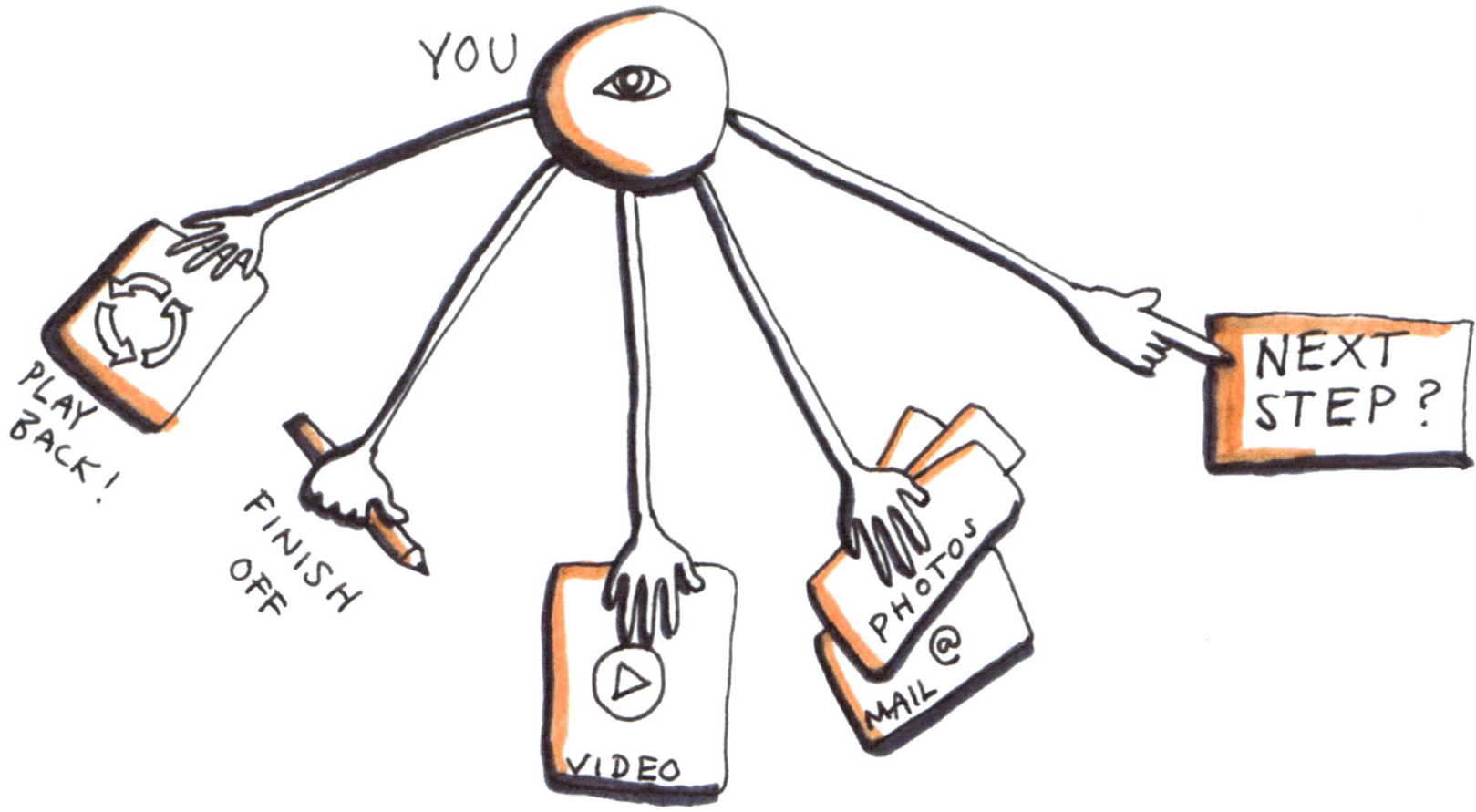

- Clarify deliverables, so both you and the client are in agreement on what must be done afterward and by whom.

- Ask for testimonials, preferably in video format. Note their names.

case studies

case 1

A group of leaders spent a weekend together with the objective of creating a clear story about common values, roles, and goals for the company's future. A perfect way to communicate this to the rest of the organization was to have a drawing done by a professional, namely me.

We began with open dialogue so the team could focus on their thoughts, the main learnings from the workshop, and which images would be the most relevant to illustrate them.

We agreed on the way to start the drawing or the "entrance" to the story, so to speak. We also decided on the different roles and how they could be described in pictures in the most clear and humoristic way.

The drawing was presented to the organization afterward at different conferences where the group of leaders urged the audience to guess who was who in the drawing as a way to generate feelings of ownership over the values and goals agreed upon.

During the image-creating process, there was laughter, aha moments, and "Yes, that is clearly us!" or "That is so typically me!" The same reaction occurred when the drawing was presented to the rest of the organization, both nationally and internationally – laughter and a feeling of "Aha, yes, we get the point, we see what you are about and who you are."

"Lise has an incredible ability to capture and visualize what is being said and the illustrations become a reflection of Chr. Hansen regarding our values and what we strive for. They also invite people to have a dialogue and to share their thoughts because it becomes so obvious what our focus is.

The graphical recording is a kind of documentation that lives for a long time in our consciousness and contributes to a strong commitment to our projects and company in general."

Susanne Grøn, Vice President, Process Innovation, Chr. Hansen

case 2

The topic of the workshop was a complex subject that the company needed to address and find a strategy for. It lasted six hours. During the workshop, different people gave their opinion on the subject and came across barriers and possibilities, and while the presentations and dialogue took place, a graphical recording was done. At the end of the day, the participants were asked to go through the drawing and emphasize the main points of the day. They had to focus on the next steps for the near future and agree upon things that could wait.

The drawing was put on the wall in a room where people involved in the project and process could see it every day. It reminded them to concentrate on the main goal and follow the project timeline without being distracted by topics that were not to be handled just yet.

Apart from that, the project became simpler to relate to and made people believe in the fact that even though it was a complex project, it was a possible task to handle and work out a plan for inviting the right people at the right time to take part.

The drawing also peaked the interest of people visiting the company and garnered positive attention. It was natural to talk about the project with the drawing as a platform for conversation.

It proves that drawing the main points and process makes things clearer for everyone to see. It makes complex themes earthy and simple, helps focus on what is most important today, and brings a touch of lightness, creativity, positivity, and joy into the work process.

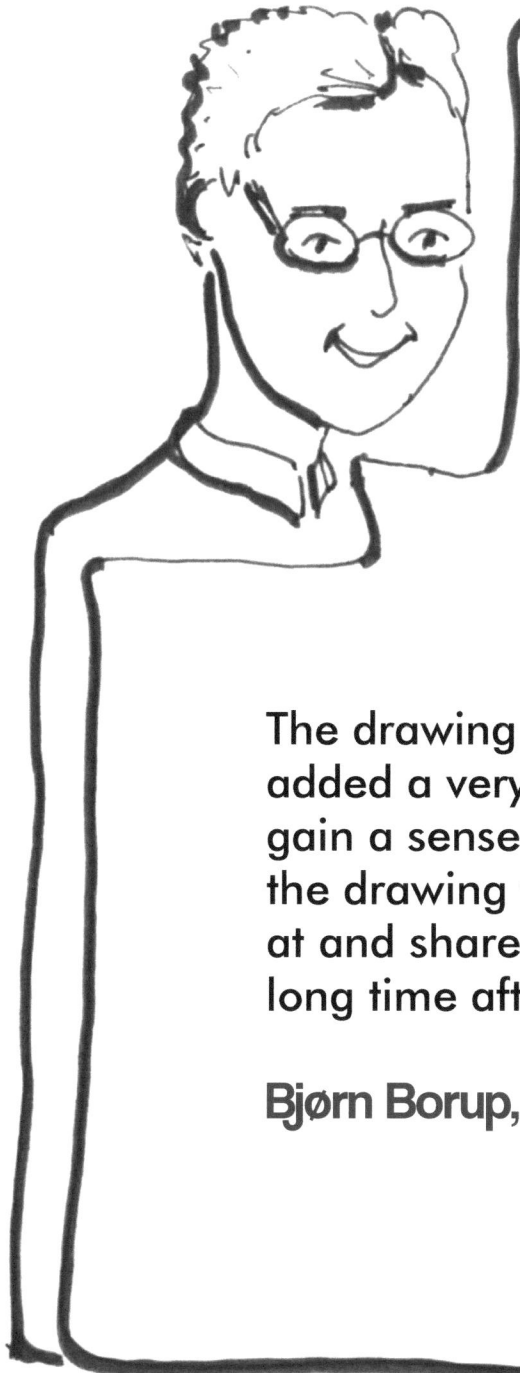

"Lise Grastrup made a graphical recording at a workshop discussing a complex subject. During the day Lise listened and drew simultaneously, and at the end of the day invited the participants to go through the drawing, focusing on the most important tasks and things to be handled here and now and by whom.

The drawing made the subject seem less complex, which added a very positive kind of focus, helping the participants gain a sense of joy and engagement for the project. AND: the drawing was put on a wall afterwards for people to look at and share thoughts and ideas, so it actually 'lived' for a long time after the actual workshop."

Bjørn Borup, CIO, Ingeniørforeningen IDA

case 3

A small company had a full day seminar to discuss their values and goals for the future, and a graphical recording was done simultaneously. The topics addressed both the culture within the company and the culture regarding their clients. Many useful points were made, and it really became apparent at the end of the day, when going through the drawing, what they ought to do more of and what could be scaled back. The company felt proud when looking at the drawing. It conveyed the idea that their company culture was very much like that of a close family with all of its good and bad sides, but mostly good.

As a fixed part of their internal weekly status meeting, they talk about the points in the drawing, reminding themselves who they want to be and what are their main values. It is a unique platform for conversation that emphasizes the great sides of the company and their employees.

The drawing is hanging in their office three years later and still brings insightful and valuable talks to the surface. One of the employees says that every now and then, when he is the last person at the office he takes a look at the drawing, and due to the fact that it is very big, his mind is smothered in the pictures and makes him reflect on where to maintain focus.

"On May 29, 2015, we at GlobalDenmark spent a full day together with the objective of outlining the company's strategy for the next 3-5 years. Extremely thought-provoking, exciting and, inevitably, complex. Potentially difficult to remember details, links, and processes at the end of the day. Not here! We had invited Lise to be with us for the entire day to record graphically what happened during the day.

The result became literally unforgettable: today, a five-meter-long series of interconnected images adorns a wall in our office, giving rise to daily reflections and discussion. Hugely valuable and aesthetically attractive. Lise did an excellent job – warmly recommended for any business event that deserves to be remembered."

Claus Jarløv, CEO, Global Denmark

about lise grastrup

Lise Grastrup is the owner of Tanke til Streg, which is Danish for "thought to line." She draws graphical recordings at workshops, conferences, and other types of events and teaches courses both online and in-person.

Lise offers a range of courses in graphic facilitation both traditional courses and online courses where you decide how fast you go.

For a number of years, Lise has taught and advised companies, both big and small. Through graphic recordings, visual presentations, info-movies, and training courses, she works with companies to help strengthen their communication with graphic facilitation. Lise also holds training courses open to the public. She has vast experience in teaching people with different needs and positions in their everyday work life.

Lise is an architect and worked for a couple of years at different architectural companies. However, she found a lack of creativity and direct use of visual interaction and communication with clients and their ideas and needs. So, in 2014 she launched her own company, Tanke til Streg, meaning "thought to line."

Stay informed and receive more guidance and tools on her website.

dedication

I would like to dedicate this book to my husband and two daughters who have supported me all the way in becoming a strong and confident businesswoman and doing what I love for a living! Hopefully, I inspire my daughters on a daily basis to go after their gut-feeling and dreams, and listen to their heart more than their brains!

Thank you, Nanna Frank and Anne Madsen. Back in 2012, I participated in your inspiring course "graphical facilitation" where you taught me the basics and opened my eyes to the great world of visual communication.

Finally, thank you, Malene Bendtsen, for making it possible to actually turn this book project into a reality. I couldn't and wouldn't have done it without your great support and your clever and beautiful mind!

www.ingramcontent.com/pod-product-compliance
Lightning Source LLC
Chambersburg PA
CBHW041226020426

42333CB00005B/63